Azure Security For Critical Workloads

Implementing Modern Security Controls for Authentication, Authorization and Auditing

Sagar Lad

Apress®

Azure Security For Critical Workloads: Implementing Modern Security Controls for Authentication, Authorization and Auditing

Sagar Lad
Navsari, India

ISBN-13 (pbk): 978-1-4842-8935-8   ISBN-13 (electronic): 978-1-4842-8936-5
https://doi.org/10.1007/978-1-4842-8936-5

Managing Director, Apress Media LLC: Welmoed Spahr
Acquisitions Editor: Smriti Srivastava
Development Editor: Laura Berendson
Coordinating Editor: Shrikant Vishwakarma
Copyeditor: Kezia Endsley

Cover designed by eStudioCalamar

Cover image by Iccup on Unsplash (www.unsplash.com)

Distributed to the book trade worldwide by Apress Media, LLC, 1 New York Plaza, New York, NY 10004, U.S.A. Phone 1-800-SPRINGER, fax (201) 348-4505, e-mail orders-ny@springer-sbm.com, or visit www.springeronline.com. Apress Media, LLC is a California LLC and the sole member (owner) is Springer Science + Business Media Finance Inc (SSBM Finance Inc). SSBM Finance Inc is a **Delaware** corporation.

For information on translations, please e-mail booktranslations@springernature.com; for reprint, paperback, or audio rights, please e-mail bookpermissions@springernature.com.

Apress titles may be purchased in bulk for academic, corporate, or promotional use. eBook versions and licenses are also available for most titles. For more information, reference our Print and eBook Bulk Sales web page at http://www.apress.com/bulk-sales.

Any source code or other supplementary material referenced by the author in this book is available to readers on GitHub (https://github.com/Apress). For more detailed information, please visit http://www.apress.com/source-code.

Printed on acid-free paper

This work is dedicated to my parents, Bharatbhai Lad and Renukaben Lad, who have always loved me unconditionally and whose good examples have taught me to work hard for the things that I aspire to achieve.

Table of Contents

About the Author

Sagar Lad is a data solution architect working with a leading multinational software company in the Netherlands. He has deep expertise in implementing data and analytics solutions for large enterprises using the cloud and artificial intelligence. He is an experienced Azure platform evangelist with a strong focus on driving cloud adoption for enterprise organizations using Microsoft Cloud solutions and offerings, with more than nine years of IT experience. He loves blogging and is an active blogger on Medium, LinkedIn, and the C# Corner developer community. He was awarded the C# Corner MVP in September of 2021 for his contributions to the developer community.

About the Technical Reviewer

 **Bhadresh Shiyal** is an Azure data architect and Azure data engineer. For the past seven years, he has been working with a large multinational IT corporation as a solutions architect. Prior to that, he spent almost a decade in private- and public-sector banks in India in various IT positions working with several Microsoft technologies. He has 18 years of IT experience, including working for two years on an international assignment from London. He has extensive experience in application design, development, and deployment. He has worked with myriad technologies, including Visual Basic, SQL Server, SharePoint, .NET MVC, O365, Azure Data Factory, Azure Databricks, Azure Synapse Analytics, Azure Data Lake Storage Gen1/Gen2, Azure SQL Data Warehouse, Power BI, Spark SQL, Scala, Delta Lake, Azure Machine Learning, Azure Information Protection, Azure .NET SDK, Azure DevOps, and more. He holds multiple Azure Certifications, including Microsoft Certified Azure Solutions Architect Expert, Microsoft Certified Azure Data Engineer Associate, Microsoft Certified Azure Data Scientist Associate, and Microsoft Certified Azure Data Analyst Associate. Bhadresh has worked as a solutions architect on large-scale Azure Data Lake implementation projects as well as data transformation projects, in addition to large-scale customized content management systems.

Preface

This book is intended for developers and IT consultants/architects who want practical insights into moving mission-critical workloads to Azure from technology and process aspects.

Over the course of the book, you will learn about the following:

1. Dimensions of cloud security and the need for having clear demarcations of security boundaries to implement Azure's defense-in-depth security architecture.

2. The intricacies of Identity and Access Management (IAM) with Azure Active Directory and deeper insights into authentication protocols, Azure AD Application Proxy, and single sign-on with practical examples.

3. Design patterns regarding the network, infrastructure, and software aspects, including the richness of security design patterns. Includes modern design concepts like software-defined networks, network segmentation, Azure Tenant Security, Container Security, application and data access, data classification, and data encryption patterns.

4. Security processes like threat modeling, security testing, and key management for complete mediation and securing the infrastructure and application deployments.

5. Automated security monitoring with advanced observability, with practical insights into how this can be implemented with Azure Monitor and Azure Sentinel.

With that said, let's get started!

CHAPTER 1

Introduction: Dimensions of Cloud Security

Cloud adoption is a strategic move that enterprises take to optimize cost, mitigate risk, create scalable infrastructures, and build enterprise-ready applications. Different organizations can adopt different depths of cloud security, depending on their best practices.

Organizations that adopt cloud-based technologies have to identify any security risks and initiate controls to keep data in the cloud secure. Organizations should take the following measures to ensure the security of their cloud services:

- Match the organization's security requirements with the cloud's security requirements

- Audit and analyze cloud security policies with a history of transparency and security-related practices

- Understand the compliance requirements and certifications that the cloud service provider requires

This chapter covers the following topics:

- History of security and the public cloud

- Cloud security boundaries and responsibilities

- Pattern-based security

- Azure's defense-in-depth security architecture

1

© Sagar Lad 2023
S. Lad, *Azure Security For Critical Workloads*, https://doi.org/10.1007/978-1-4842-8936-5_1

History of Public Cloud Security

In the world of cloud computing, cloud solutions are ever-evolving. Organizations should ask themselves the following questions before moving to a cloud-ready environment:

- Does our organization have a security architecture in place?

- Does our organization have a future security roadmap?

- Does our organization have a security process to remediate security vulnerabilities?

If the answer to all three questions is yes, then your organization must have considered security very thoroughly and must belong to the small percentage of companies that focus on security. The bad news is that this approach could need a major overhaul when your organization decides to leverage cloud computing services.

Traditional security in the IT world was implemented from the mindset of limiting access boundaries to applications. In traditional security architectures, security controls resided in the data center and applications lived happily under the protection of the data center. Organizations had complete control of the data center and could operate the security controls the way they wanted in terms of racks, cables, rooms, and access to comply with security policies. This required proper management.

More often than not, reluctance to move to public cloud architectures is due to the fear of giving up data centers rather than any other rational cost benefits. The fear of not being able to trust someone else is understandable. And even with organizations that are brave enough to go ahead, the estimation provided by the engineers to implement new security controls can seem like a gigantic investment, as it also must include the cost of procuring new tools, teaching new skills, and implementing the system.

Risk assessment needs to be based on the organization's risk appetite, so it can evaluate which security controls could live in a public cloud. Normally, when organizations perform this exercise, it is an eye-opener and more often than not the gaps are really wide. Most traditional security controls are not applicable to risk assessment, as the parameterization in the public cloud is not as strong as with traditional or on-premises data centers.

Enterprises are rapidly moving toward cloud technology and cloud services. This trend will only increase in the coming future. Cloud computing is not the future anymore; it is already everywhere, although most end users don't even realize it. In the cloud computing world, security policies need to change their focus from "controlling access" to "protecting data".

In the cloud computing world, security requirements around data include the following:

- Confidential information must be encrypted in a secure manner

- PII (personally identifiable information) data must be protected

- Data integrity must be maintained

- Secure data disposal must be built in a mature manner

- A data lifecycle must be followed to ensure proper data usage

In cloud computing, two security controls become more important than ever before. The first is certificate management. It plays a very important role in all web service security solutions. Organizations need to make sure that they can create, renew, and revoke certificates from a central place in no time. The requirements to use the Public Key Infrastructure (PKI) must be well established, understood, and followed. The other control is Identity and Access Management (IAM), which has become the most important security control in the cloud computing world, where a lot of solutions like OpenID Connect (OIDC), Security Assertion Markup Language (SAML), and Open Authentication (OAuth) exist.

With cloud computing, security breaches can happen easily at multiple levels of technology. Therefore, defense-in-depth and complete mediation are the most important principles to follow. For business leaders, it's hard to know whether a cloud service is secure enough for their IT applications to work accurately. Business leaders have to trust their cloud providers in this regard. But security is a shared responsibility, and no cloud provider will provide a full guarantee for securing the workloads. The shared responsibility is the very reason that security architecture needs to be reconstructed in the view of risk assessments for the cloud computing model. See Figure 1-1.

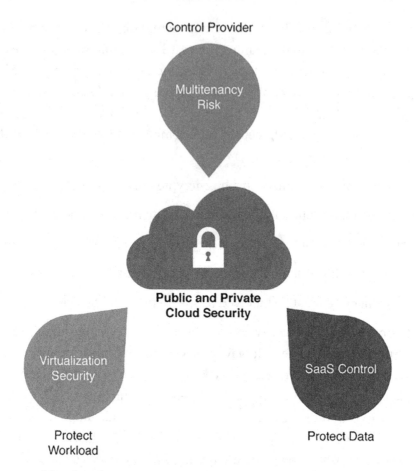

Figure 1-1. *Public cloud security*

In a nutshell, cloud computing growth has been truly astonishing and it will continue to grow in the future. Although cloud computing has many benefits, it doesn't reduce existing network security risks.

- Security risks threaten the data center and network change once the applications move to the cloud. Such security risk remains. For example, data center applications use a wide range of ports that make traditional security considerations ineffective when those applications move to the cloud. See Figure 1-2.

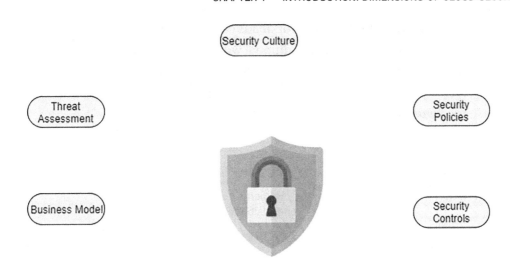

Figure 1-2. *Network security*

- Cloud computing works on the model of shared resources. It is best to separate mission-critical applications and data applications into secure network segments. This separation is also known as *zero trust segmentation*. See Figure 1-3. It is very straightforward to implement zero trust segmentation on a physical network of the enterprise data center using firewalls and virtual LANs based on the application and user identity. However, in a cloud computing environment, direct communication between the virtual machines occurs constantly. This makes the segmentation task difficult since cloud computing works on the concept of shared resources.

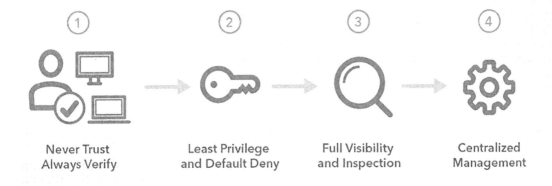

Figure 1-3. *Zero trust security*

- In cloud computing, virtual workloads can be modified in seconds/minutes. But in a traditional workload, security and other configurations can take hours. This imbalance causes problems in security policy and workload deployment during cloud migration. See Figure 1-4.

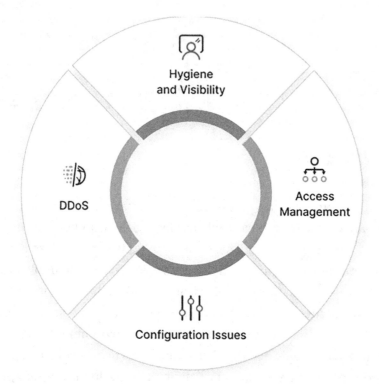

Figure 1-4. *Cloud security configurations*

When you dive deeper into cloud security considerations, you see that it is basically a shared responsibility between the cloud providers and the customers. In a shared responsibility model, there are three main categories:

- Completely the provider's responsibility: Securing the infrastructure as well as patching the compute resources

- Completely the customer's responsibility: Managing users and access privilege, preventing unauthorized access to the data, encrypting data and protecting cloud resources

- Responsibilities that differ based on the cloud service model are as follows (see Figure 1-5):

  – Infrastructure as a Service

  – Software as a Service

  – Platform as a Service

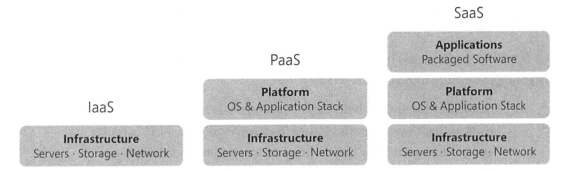

Figure 1-5. *Cloud security shared responsibility models*

Considering the popularity of the public cloud, you should be aware of these common cloud security challenges:

- Increased surface attack: Public cloud environments are more vulnerable to surface attacks by hackers and a poorly designed cloud security solution can disrupt the cloud workload.

- Lack of transparency: Public cloud providers have full control over the complete infrastructure in the IaaS model. This leads to a lack of transparency toward the end customers and is also extended to the PaaS and SaaS models.

- Dynamic cloud workload: Cloud environments are very dynamic and constantly changing at scale and with velocity. Traditional security tools are static in nature and not capable of enforcing security policies in flexible and dynamic environments.

- DevSecOps and automation: Enterprise organizations started adapting the highly automated DevOps CI/CD culture to ensure that all security controls were in place and embedded in the form of code to ensure the development lifecycle. Once the workload is deployed to production, security-related changes can have cause security concerns and increased time to market if the DevOps process is not followed.

- Granular access management: Cloud user roles cannot be configured loosely and grant more privileges than what is required. An example is giving database delete or write permissions to users who don't need such privileges.

- Cloud governance and compliance: All public cloud providers are aligned with well-known governance and compliance programs but customers are also responsible for ensuring that the workload, the data lifecycle, and its processes are compliant.

Now that you've read about these cloud security challenges, it's time to explore the six pillars of creating robust cloud security:

- Granular IAM and authentication controls: It is recommended to work with groups and roles rather than with individual IAM access. You need to grant only the minimal access privileges to assets and APIs for the group. It is best to proactively manage IAM access with strong password policies, permissions, and so on.

- Zero-trust network security control: It is advised to deploy business-critical resources in a logically isolated area of the cloud provider's network, such as virtual private cloud or virtual private network. Use subnet to micromanage the traffic between the workloads.

- Compliance to change-management process and software updates: Cloud security vendors provide robust cloud security posture management to apply governance and compliance rules when provisioning the servers.

- Secure application with a web firewall: A firewall will granularly inspect and control traffic to and from the web application servers and automatically update Web Application Firewall (WAF) rules in response to traffic changes.

- Data protection: Improved data protection with encryption at all transport layers, secure file shares and communications, risk management, maintaining secure storage of data, and so on, should be considered.

Table 1-1. *Data Protection Principles*

Lawfulness, fairness and transparency	Personal data shall be processed lawfully, fairly and in a transparent manner in relation to the data subject
Purpose limitation	Personal data shall be collected for specified, explicit and legitimate purposes and not further processed in a manner that is incompatible with those purposes
Data minimisation	Personal data shall be adequate, relevant and limited to what is necessary in relation to the purposes for which they are processed
Accuracy	Personal data shall be accurate and, where necessary, kept up to date
Storage limitation	Personal data shall be kept in a form which permits identification of data subjects for no longer than is necessary for the purposes for which the personal data are processed
Integrity and confidentiality	Personal data shall be processed in a manner that ensures appropriate security of the personal data, including protection against unauthorised or unlawful processing and against accidental loss, destruction or damage, using appropriate technical or organisational measures
Accountability	The controller shall be responsible for, and be able to demonstrate compliance with the GDPR

- Threat intelligence: Third-party cloud security vendors work by collecting all the cloud-native logs with internal data, such as asset and configuration management systems, and vulnerability detection, as well as external data such as threat intelligence feeds, and so on. They also provide tools to visualize and query the landscape and incident response times. Real-time alerts about policy violations shorten time to remediation. There are various types of intelligence threats, as highlighted in Figure 1-6.

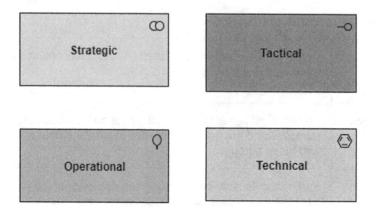

Figure 1-6. *Threat intelligence types*

Cloud Security Boundaries and Responsibilities

Decoding what "cloud-ready application" means is like opening a can of worms. First of all, there are no basic steps, as it's still a new topic and can depend on assumptions and opinionated views. If you Google "cloud-ready" it's sometimes defined as "designing applications for the Internet". Well, frankly that's like saying "a car is designed for the road". Although this is not wrong, such definitions are not helpful, as it is hard to write any requirements with this explanation.

Given the evolution in technology today, being "cloud-ready" could be as simple as containerizing an application and hosting it over a managed infrastructure. While this is partially correct, cross-cutting concerns like security and resiliency are the ones that create havoc in the quest to become cloud-ready. The scope of cloud-ready does look small and manageable at first, but the further down it goes, the bigger it gets.

Cloud-ready applications adhere to the following three principles (see Figure 1-7):

- The infrastructure must no longer be perceived as a bunch of physical boxes of hardware, but rather a bunch of managed services. In the cloud-ready world, an infrastructure platform is an integrated set of equipment, operating software, middleware, databases, and centralized services that help the applications run seamlessly.

- The infrastructure platform includes the provisioning, hardening, and configuration of the platform services and is based on easily-scalable, hyperconverged infrastructure. The infrastructure platform must be easily reproducible and leverage the Infrastructure as Code (IaC).

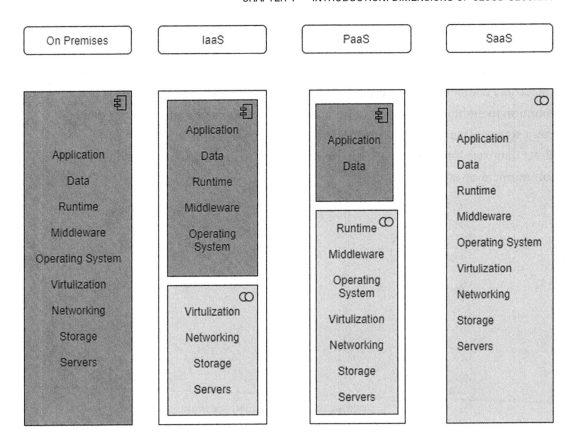

Figure 1-7. *Cloud security boundaries*

- To enhance IT resiliency, applications must be written to allow failures and handle these gracefully without loss of service. Failure on the cloud is inevitable, so applications that are truly cloud-ready must be designed for failures. Such applications are far more capable of self-healing, restarting, and continuing operational services when the worst happens. This is more than just a disaster recovery plan. Applications must have been thoughtful about failure modes like hardware failures, operating system failures, Internet failures, network peering issues, and other aspects that may be outside their direct control. They must still be able to handle these gracefully and automatically.

These are possible by embracing new resilience patterns like retry, circuit breakers, Command and Query Responsibility Segregation (CQRS), sharding, and many more. Technology architecture plays an important role here, by designing systems that are loosely coupled, auditable, and based on proven resilience patterns. It is also common to embrace principles of microservices for application development and event sourcing via immutable events for auditing. In addition, any file sharing or direct database interactions need to be replaced with asynchronous or synchronous communication styles.

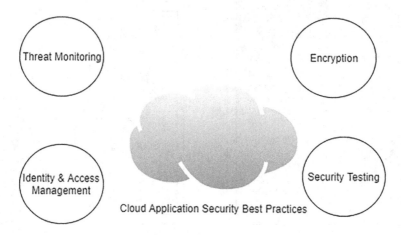

Figure 1-8. *Cloud application security best practices*

Traditional security controls are not enough and security architecture needs revamping. Traditional security was implemented from the mindset of limiting access boundaries toward the applications.

In cloud-ready architectures, the perimeters for access boundaries are much looser and new security controls need to be implemented. Two security controls become more important than ever before:

- The first is certificate management and it plays a significant role in all web service security solutions. Organizations need to make sure that they can create, renew, and revoke certificates from a central place in no time. The requirements for use of the PKI must be well established and understood.

- The other control is Identity and Access Management (IAM), which has become the most important security control in the cloud computing world, where a lot of solutions like OIDC, SAML, and OAuth exist.

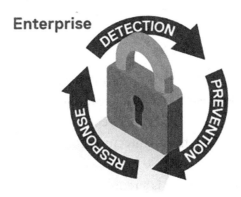

Figure 1-9. *Traditional application security*

These three pointers highlight where energy and design efforts need to go to create a cloud-ready enterprise application. More importantly, a cloud-ready organization also needs a cultural change, which includes embracing new skills. To begin, your organization needs a good vision and strategy. Such transformations can take time. Just like it takes a whole village to raise a baby, it will take the whole organization to become cloud-ready!

Pattern-Based Security

We often talk about modern principles like infrastructure as code, microservices for applications, service-oriented approaches with enterprise bus, and so on. How often do we underestimate the work that needs to go into these principles?

In the good old days, the simple architecture of the client-server database was centralized. Its simplicity was the key to keeping it running in a confined network space. Access was controlled using simple firewalls and login passwords with basic authentication.

Figure 1-10 shows how to identify the list of threats for each asset and identify the controls that mitigate each threat. Once the assets are identified, the next step is to create an asset-centric access list for each asset.

For each asset   Create a list threat for each asset   Controls which mitigate each threat   Create asset centric access control list

Figure 1-10. *Cloud security pattern*

These worked brilliantly in the 1990s, as connections were small and distribution was not a requirement, but a wish. The challenge in those days was about balancing cost to meet timelines rather than dealing with complexity. Architecture was not in the limelight, as more often than not, the architecture would just be a few flows in a client-server database set.

Times have changed. Distribution is a requirement and delimiting access is not considered a smart thing to do. Today, client-server-databases are considered an anti-pattern to modernization. Speaking about client-server-databases sounds like the 1990s.

Today's architecture needs to be built on high-level principles of scalability, with the core requirements to protect data and allow access in a controlled fashion. The needs of a scalable architecture are moving to a pluggable interface, where ubiquity is the norm. Client-server, microservices, and service-oriented architecture all work together brilliantly well in a pluggable way in hybrid cloud models. But to do this, the architecture roots have to be very strong, and security is one of the biggest pillars of this foundation. See Figure 1-11.

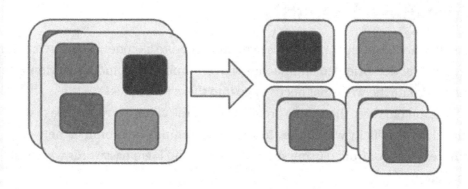

Figure 1-11. *Monolithic vs microservice architecture*

A fundamental part of a scalable, modernized architecture is pattern-based security. This is fundamental for companies looking at a hybrid cloud model, as networking partitions will blur over time and applications are becoming more accessible and vulnerable than in the 1990s.

Pattern-based security is based on the fundamentals of compartmentalization with security zones. The compartmentalization is logical and achieved with security dimensions. As a simple example, assume you have a very simple service-oriented architecture with three layers—a consumer, an API gateway, and a provider. The layers are one security dimension. Then comes the famous CIA (Confidentiality, Integrity, and Availability) ratings, which is another security dimension. Another security dimension is the consumer type, internal or external. Based on your organization, more security dimensions could be added. See Figure 1-12.

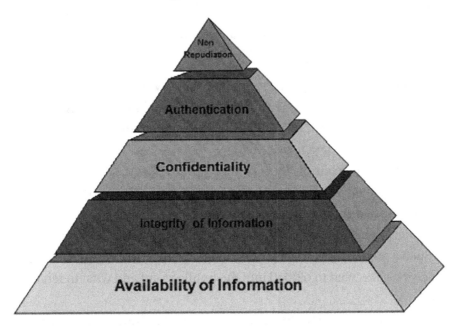

Figure 1-12. *Security dimensions*

Continuing from the security dimensions already discussed (layers, CIA rating, and consumer type), try to map them to security zones:

Layer; CIA; Consumer type; Computed Security zone

Consumer;111; Internal; Extra Small

API gateway;111; Internal; Medium

Provider; 111; Internal; Large

This table can go on, to an enterprise security model. What is important is that it is clear how many security zones you need. As a rule of thumb, there should not be more than ten security zones.

To build on the story further, every security zone must be mapped to security controls. The security controls must be based on the risk-based policies of the organization. (For example, an application with confidential data may need a firewall, encryption, and an authentication and access control list, but another application without data may only need the security control of the firewall.) Continuing from the fictitious example, you could translate this to the following mapping of security zones and security controls:

1. Extra small security zone - Firewall

2. Medium security zone - Firewall + Encrypt

3. Large security zone - Firewall + Encrypt + Authentication + Access Control List

The aforementioned security zones and their security controls are only examples. A real example of any medium-to-large enterprise would include more. (At rare times, it could be more than ten zones. If this is the case, the architecture may be very complex due to other reasons not related to security.)

Each of these security controls must be then governed with security policies and rich sets of standards, guidelines, and acceptance criteria, probably also dash-boarded to show the weak points of the application landscape.

Such a model is a holistic approach toward pattern-based security and has rich scalability. Such a model allows decision-making toward a hybrid cloud strategy, enabling decisions like what to offload into the public cloud and what to retain in private data centers.

Pattern-based security is a prerequisite of any scalable, modernized architecture. It keeps the complexity in control and still leads to a complete mediation. In addition, such a strong foundation with pattern-based security enables higher management to make strategic decisions on the future of data centers and, more importantly, estimate costs better.

In addition to understanding pattern-based security, you need to understand the software layers that create a scalable application security model for moving to a distributed architecture. See Figure 1-13.

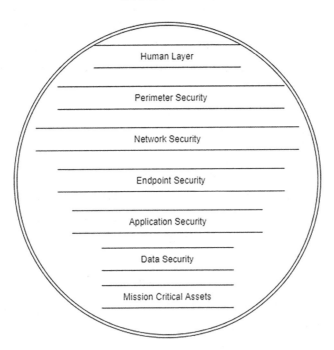

Figure 1-13. *Security layers*

The speed of digitalization creates the urge and need to be ready for the next phase of execution, which consists of heterogeneous integration flows. Decoupling the architecture from static dependencies is becoming the most important characteristic for the survival of the organization. Decoupling creates the flexibility to replace applications or legacy systems, but also to scale quickly and to monitor and guarantee overall security. One aspect that's a beautiful practice is embracing software layering. The number of layers is not important, but the architecture principles per layer is really important. The principles for application layers are as follows:

- A centralized integration layer to decouple the service consumers and service providers. The integration layer must be responsible for message routing, transformation, and mediation.

- Multiple consumer layers that are equivalent to the demand for consumable services and more often than not have a user interface with presentation views. No databases must be hosted in the consumer layer and no two consumers could have a data flow.

- Multiple provider layers are responsible for delivering services that consist of heavy lifting business logic, statefulness, and persistence. Any provider service must be exposed as services in the integration layer.

Consumer Layer

The consumer layer hosts consumer applications that create business value with personalized, engaging, and interactive experiences. These interactions can be for a single screen type use or can involve multiple viewports and devices to present the functionality in fit-for-purpose Human Machine Interface (HMI).

While consumer applications are responsible for service functional needs, from non-functional aspects, the consumer layer also increases availability and resilience by coping with failures to backend systems. An important element of any consumer application is gracefully handling exceptions, while decreasing response times by using in-memory caching and content delivery networks.

The consuming layer application must have a faster time to market. The consumer layer application must not hold any persistence.

Integration Layer

The integration layer is the decoupling layer and must be composed of either one or polyglot technologies that serve as the only gateway for exchange of data flows between the service consumer to the service provider. The integration layer must also provide a minimal set of capabilities to enable service providers and service consumers to interact.

When the service provider is outside the organization, the integration layer can also hold data in persistence storage.

The integration layer provides standardized ways of message routing, transformation, and mediation in order to expose enterprise services.

The integration layer can safeguard quality, assure the overall architecture, and apply security controls.

An integration layer must be mapped to a separate security zone and controls. As an example, an integration layer must use client certificates to safeguard the integrity and confidentiality of the provider applications.

The interface layer is only responsible for interfaces and hence can be a place to standardize the standards. In today's world, the SOAP (XML), REST, and JSON standards are the most common.

As integration layer is not an implementation layer, so no heavy business logic should reside in it.

In order to protect the unintended flow of information to consumers, the integration layer is also responsible for security controls like the access control list and encryption in addition to other basic requirements, like routing and throttling (rate limiting). These security controls should be formulated based on the business needs.

The integration layer can also act as a stitching layer for legacy-consuming applications that require any form of integration or transformation.

Provider Layer

Provider layer applications provide data and business functionality.

A provider layer application must shield the data and business logic, as these are the core of any business. The provider layer should not provide the integration layer with direct access to the databases, rather the databases must be wrapped by reusable services.

Based on the needs of the business, the provider layer component could host a database for persistence. In today's DevOps world, established, open source database solutions prevent a potentially costly vendor lock-in and allow companies to benefit from the input of the open source community. Many open source databases are available in the market, with SQL and NoSQL flavors like MongoDB and Cassandra.

The provider application must be based on the principle of reusability and must be atomic for the functionality it provides.

Provider services, which then depend on other provider services, can introduce static dependencies, which need to be avoided and will otherwise increase the complexity of the overall architecture.

Linking Software Layers to Application Security

The previous introduction to software layers can make it much easier to apply pattern-based security, following principles like defense-in-depth and complete mediation, yet still keeping security easy and scalable.

For any organization that's taking the leap to distributed architecture, putting software layers in place and leveraging pattern-based security will reap a lot of benefits and improve the lifetime and agility of the organization.

Azure's Defense-in-Depth Security Architecture

Defense-in-depth is a security risk management approach that defines multiple security layers in an IT environment, so that if a security attack is not caught by one layer, it will more likely be caught by another layer. Multiple security layers increase the overall security score of an environment and reduce the probability of a security breach.

With the rapid expansion of cloud computing, requirements for a defense-in depth strategy have increased dramatically. Cloud security is a shared responsibility between the customer and the cloud provider. Let's consider each security layer with respect to Azure:

- Physical security: Microsoft has its own Azure data centers and manages physical security at all locations. Only authorized persons should have access to different areas of the data centers. See Figure 1-14.

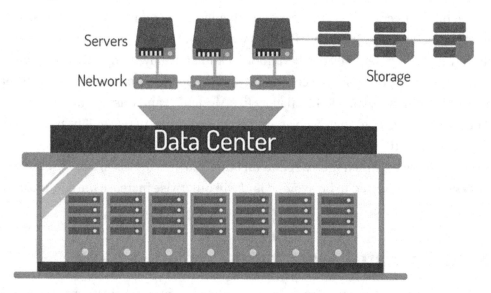

Figure 1-14. *Physical data centers*

- Identity and Access: All Azure resources are governed and controlled through the Azure Active Directory, which is the central place to manage all identities and related access. In addition to this, you can also manage access using role-based access controls. Certain users can also be assigned just-in time access to certain services to make it more secure using the Azure Privileged Identity management. See Figure 1-15.

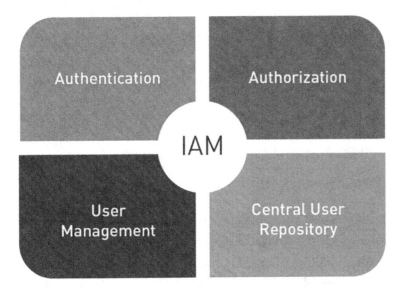

Figure 1-15. *Identity and access management with Azure AD*

- Perimeter: By default, Azure enables basic distributed denial of service, which comes with traffic monitoring and real-time mitigation of the network attacks. The standard tier of the DDoS provides additional capabilities to protect volumetric attacks.

- Network: You can filter network traffic from the Azure resources in a virtual network through the Network Security Groups (NSGs), which contain security rules allowing or denying traffic.

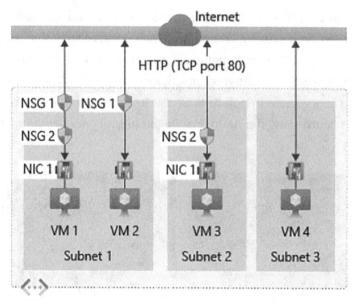

Figure 1-16. *Virtual network*

- Application Gateway: Application gateway and the web application firewall provide the centralized protection of the web application from vulnerabilities. Managed Identity from the Azure Active Directory allows the app to easily access the Azure Active Directory resources, such as Azure Key Vault.

- Data: Data is encrypted-at-rest for both structured and unstructured data. Using a combination of Azure Active Directory and Azure Key Vault, data can be encrypted and stored securely.

Looking back at the Open Systems Interconnection (OSI) model, there are seven layers. Possible threats and security measures can be applied to mitigate/control the threats.

OSI Layer	Protocols*	Used for	Possible threats	Security measures
Application Layer	Telnet, FTP, SMTP, DHCP, HTTP, SNMP, SMPP	Interaction at the user end with applications.	Backdoor attacks, static passwords, SNMP Private Community Strings	· Authentication/Access Control · Virus scanners · TLS encryption
Presentation Layer	XDR, TLS, SSL , MIME	Encryption and Decryption	Virus, worms	· Cryptographic Algorithm · Input Validation
Session Layer	PPTP, RPC, SAP, L2TP, NetBIOS	Create a session between 2 nodes for efficient exchange of data.	Personal information retrieval, root privilege access, Net Bios attacks, RPC Attacks	· Session Management
Transport Layer	TCP, UDP, IPX/SPX, DCCP, SCTP	This layer transmits data from source to destination node.	Endpoint identification, unauthorized Internet access , SYN flood, Ping of death.	· Private IP addressing via Network Address Translation (NAT) · Firewalls
Network Layer	IPv4, IPv6, IPX, AppleTalk, ICMP, IPSec, IGMP	Real time processing and transfers data from nodes to nodes		· Router Access Control Lists · Demilitarized zone (DMZ) · Proxy/ Application gateway
Data Link Layer	ARP, CSLIP, HDLC, IEEE.802.3, PPP, X-25, SLIP, ATM, SDLS, PLIP	Transforms the digital signals into frames.	ARP spoofing, MAC flooding, Spanning tree attack, 802.1Q and ISL tagging attack	· Tunneling · VPN connections
Physical Layer	Bluetooth, PON, OTN, DSL, IEEE.802.11, IEEE.802.3, L431, TIA 449	Hardware of networks such as cabling to transmit the digital signals.	Power loss or power spikes	· Uninterruptible power supply (UPS)

Figure 1-17. *Security layers, protocols, and possible threats*

Implementing security at every OSI layer will never protect against all cyberattacks. But the more the layers that are protected, the more hardened your application and system are from unintentional mishaps. Security is a continuous beast and it needs to be looked on with discipline and knowledge in order to close up any new open holes.

Although it is rather hard to project cost to implementing security measures, it should be done from a business mindset. This implies that mission-critical applications and data need to be better protected, as they can put an enterprise out of business; this risk should be addressed.

Conclusion

This chapter explored the various dimensions of cloud security. It explored in detail the history of security and the public cloud. It also took a deep dive into the boundaries and responsibilities to be considered when adopting cloud security. You also learned about the need for pattern-based security and about Azure's defense-in-depth security architecture.

This next chapter explains how to configure Identity and Access Management using Azure Active Directory with various features.

CHAPTER 2

Identity and Access Management with Azure Active Directory

Identity and access management (IAM) is the process of authenticating and authorizing security principles. Enterprises should govern and configure identity and access management to make sure that services, applications, users, and groups have correct access to data.

Azure Active Directory is an enterprise identity service that provides single sign-on (SSO), multifactor authentication (MFA), and conditional access to protect against security attacks.

This chapter covers the following topics:

- Identity protocols and application types

- Azure Active Directory security model

- Active directory federation services

- Azure AD Application Proxy

- Azure AD B2B and B2C for external partners

- PIM Azure AD Identity protection hybrid implementation

- Single sign-on with Azure AD

© Sagar Lad 2023
S. Lad, *Azure Security For Critical Workloads*, https://doi.org/10.1007/978-1-4842-8936-5_2

Identity Protocol and Application Types

Microsoft Azure has an identity platform that allows developers to build different types of applications for various business needs. They can create single page applications, web applications, mobile apps, and services.

Single Page Applications

In recent years, web applications have become more popular and so advanced that developers can create sophisticated client applications. These client-side applications are also known as single sided page applications (SPA).

Let's look at how to create, configure, and use Azure AD applications to use the data returned from Microsoft Graph with the OAuth 2.0 protocol.

Modern web applications are written in languages like Vue, React, and Angular. The easiest way to use Microsoft Identity for authentication purposes is to obtain access tokens to authorize requests and secure endpoints.

First, a single page application has to be registered as a new app using Azure AD. This does the authentication and obtains access tokens using Microsoft Graph. Once the application is created using Azure AD, you configure it with the single page application. You can do this by using the Azure AD Admin Center at `https://aad.portal.azure.com`, as shown in Figure 2-1.

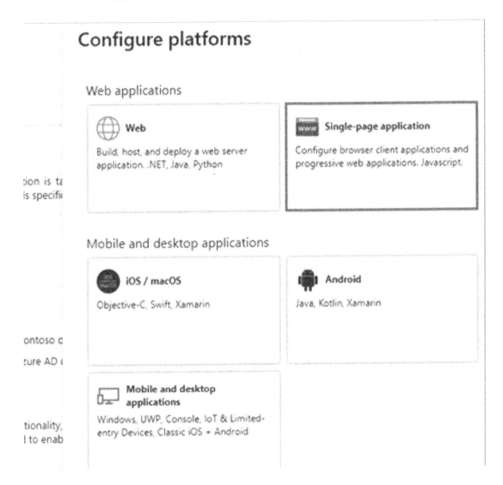

Figure 2-1. *Azure AD app registration*

Once the Azure AD application is configured, you have to make sure that the redirect URI of the app points to the URL of the SPA. See Figure 2-2.

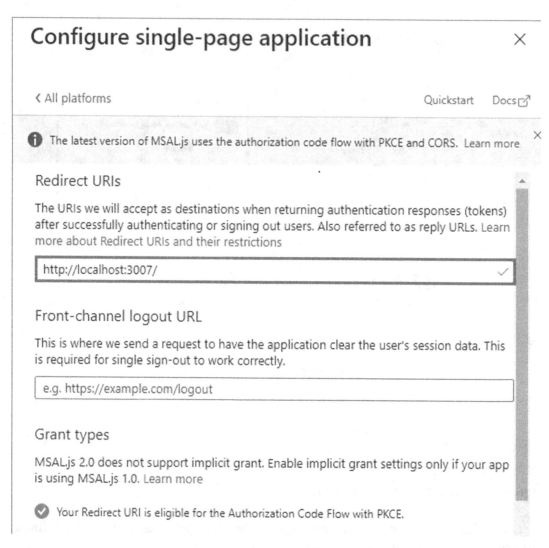

Figure 2-2. *Azure AD single page app configuration*

Web Apps with Sign In and API Calling

Developers can use Microsoft Identity to add authentication to a web app and require users to sign in to the web application. Once users are signed in and the user grants consent, the web application will obtain a token from Azure AD and use it to request data from the web APIs. In the second phase, you can enable the application to call the web API on behalf of the single sign-on users.

OAuth 2.0 authorization code grant flow: OAuth 2.0 authorization code flow is common when websites or custom applications use Azure AD as a federated authentication provider. When the application wants users to sign in or needs access to the token, it redirects users using Azure AD authentication. See Figure 2-3.

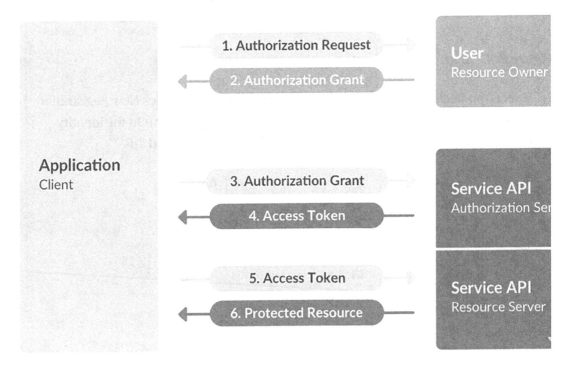

Figure 2-3. *OAuth 2.0 Flow*

As shown in Figure 2-3, the application client will create an authorization request to the user or resource owner. Once the resource owner receives the request, it will grant authorization. Clients then accept the authorization using the service API, which will then generate an access token. Based on the access token, the service provider will protect the resource and serve the client request.

The next step is to create a server-side web application that will allow users to sign in and grant the app permission to act on behalf of the end user.

Now you create a single tenant Azure AD application. From the Azure Portal, select Azure Active Directory. See Figure 2-4.

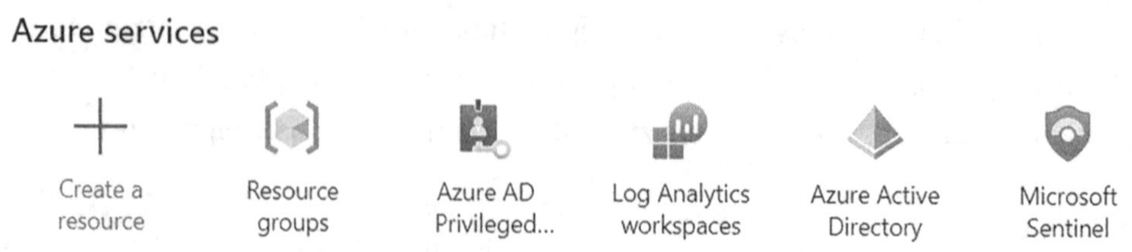

Azure services

Create a resource	Resource groups	Azure AD Privileged...	Log Analytics workspaces	Azure Active Directory	Microsoft Sentinel

Figure 2-4. *Azure Active Directory*

Select App Registration from the Azure Active Directory and click New Registration. Then provide a name and the account type to create an application. On the identity page, select the application ID and directory ID. See Figures 2-5 and 2-6.

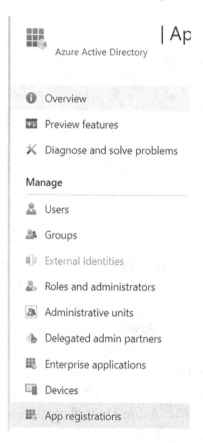

Figure 2-5. *Azure Active Directory app registration*

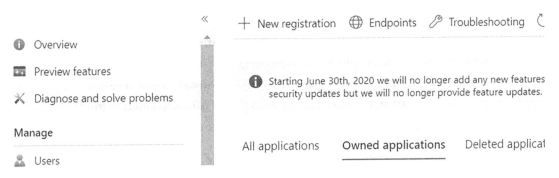

Figure 2-6. *Azure Active Directory new app registration*

With OAuth 2.0, four parties are typically involved in the authentication and authorization exchange. When such authentication or authorization happens, the flows are called *authentication flows* or *auth flows*. See Figure 2-7.

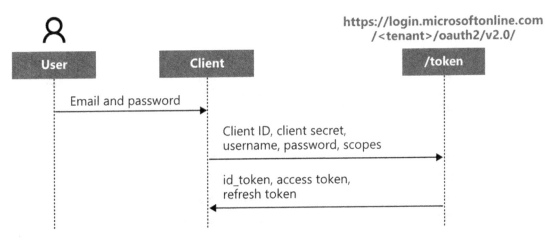

Figure 2-7. *Authentication flow*

- Authorization server: The Microsoft Identity platform, also known as IdP or the identity provider, handles the end user information, related access, and the relationship between the requestor and server for the authentication flow. The server generates the security tokens to grant, deny, or revoke access to the resources.

- Client: In OAuth, clients are generally end users or applications that request access to a protected resource. Clients can be end users or an applications that are requesting access to the resource.

- Resource owner: In the authentication flow, the resource owner is typically an end user that owns the protected resources and data on your behalf. For example, if you want to get information from the Azure Active Directory using the Graph API, you can create a service principal in Azure AD with the required permissions to call the graph API to find the relevant information. See Figure 2-8.

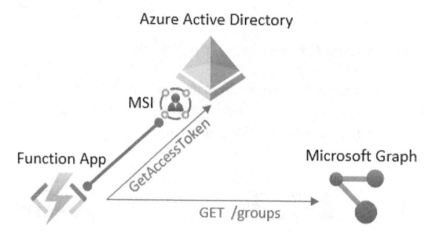

Figure 2-8. *Azure AD Graph API*

- Resource server: The resource server provides access to the resource's own data. It is a web API that relies on authorization to perform the authentication from bearer tokens that are issued by the authorization server. This grants the required access to the resources.

During the OAuth flow, there are various tokens involved in the communication. These tokens are used to ensure, verify, and grant/deny access to the protected resource. There are three types of bearer tokens used by Microsoft Identity Platform:

- Access tokens: Access tokens are generated and issued by the authorization server to the client application. These access tokens contain the permissions that clients have requested to access the specific resources. See Figure 2-9.

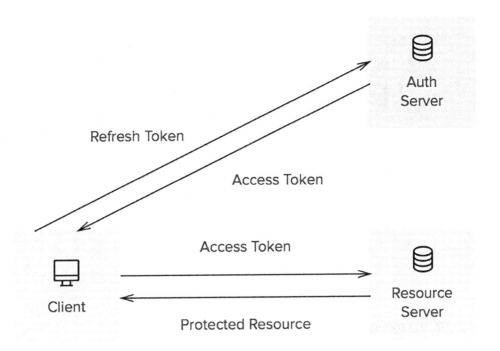

Figure 2-9. *Access tokens*

- ID tokens: They are used by the authorization server. When the end
  users or clients try to sign in, the server will gather basic information
  about the users to serve the client requests. See Figure 2-10.

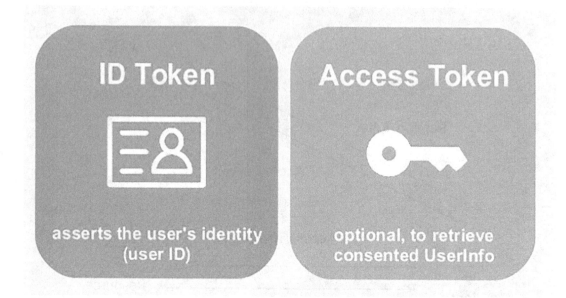

Figure 2-10. *ID tokens*

- Refresh tokens: End users and clients use refresh tokens to request new access tokens or ID tokens from the authorization servers. See Figure 2-11.

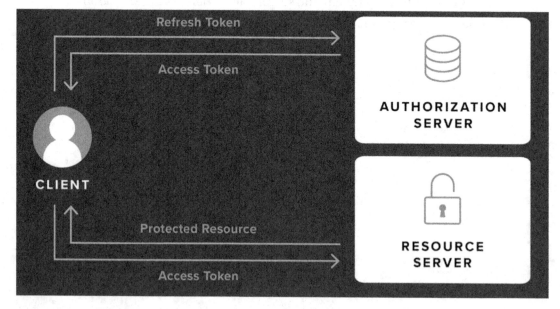

Figure 2-11. *Refresh tokens*

Azure Active Directory Security Model

Azure Active Directory plays a very important role in defining the strategy of identity and access management. It helps scale the solution, save on costs, and improve the overall security. Organizations must use a combination of on-premises and cloud-only accounts so that users can access both types of accounts. Managing users, applications, and access on both on-premises and on cloud has major challenges.

Azure Active Directory creates common user identities for authentication and authorization to all Azure resources, which is known as the *hybrid identity*. There are three methods for creating the hybrid identity:

- Password hash synchronization

- Passthrough authentication

- Federation

Let's go through a checklist to deploy the recommended actions to secure organizations:

1. Make strong credentials.

2. Reduce areas to attack.

3. Automate the threat response.

4. Use cloud intelligence.

5. Enable self-service.

An identity assessment score is an automated assessment of the Azure AD tenant's identity security configuration. Your identity secure score reflects how well your organization is aligned with Microsoft's best practice recommendations. See Figure 2-12.

Figure 2-12. *Azure AD identity score*

This identity score helps you achieve the following:

- Measure identity security posture

- Identify and list security improvements

- Measure the success of your security improvements

Let's now look at the best security practices for Azure AD in detail.

Make Strong Credentials

There are various types of attacks happening that impact your software applications. They can include phishing attacks, consent phishing, and password-based attacks.

In order to prevent these attacks, it is recommended to enable multifactor authentication for your application and make sure that your credentials are strong. In order to easily enable a basic level of the identity security, you can use the one-click enablement with Azure AD's security defaults. See Figure 2-13.

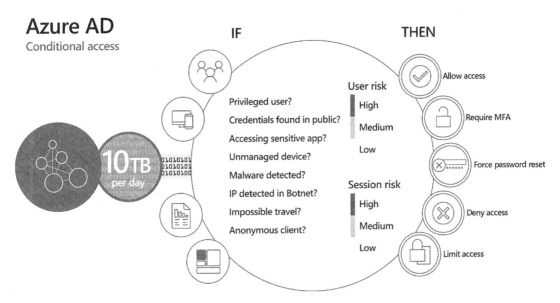

Figure 2-13. *Azure AD security defaults*

This security default ensures that you can enable Azure AD MFA for the tenant users and blocks the sign in using the traditional protocol. Many organizations use complex password expiration rules. As per the standard recommendations, it is advised to use Azure AD password protection, which is a dynamic banned password feature that prevents users from setting passwords that are easy to guess. See Figure 2-14.

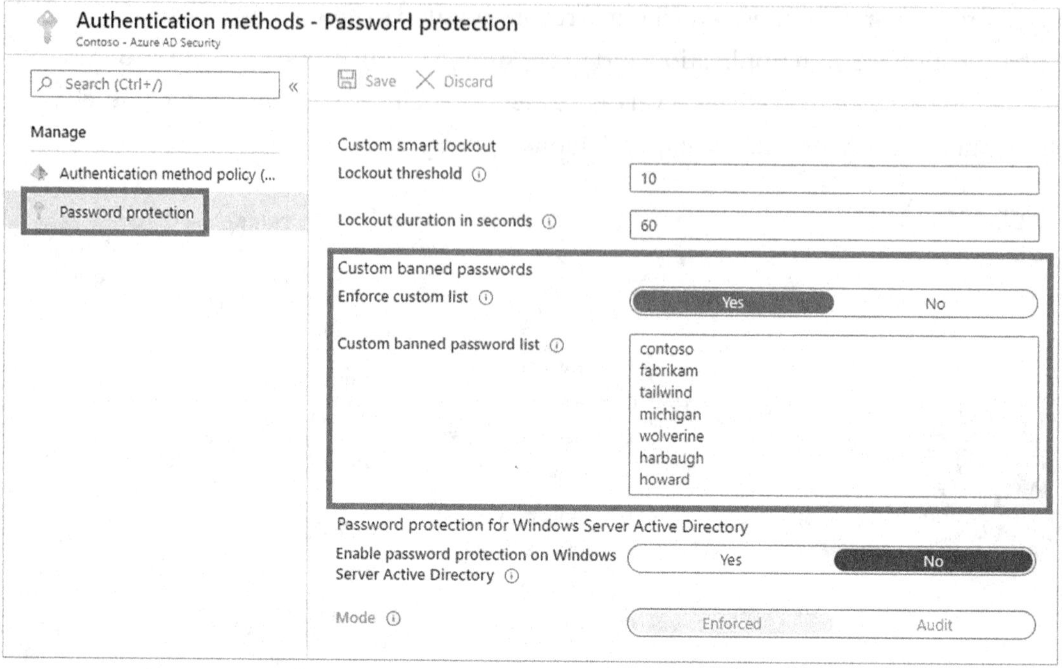

Figure 2-14. *Azure AD password protection*

There are two types of banned password lists:

- Global banned password list

- Custom banned password list

  - Brand names

  - Product names

  - Locations such cities and headquarters

  - Company-specific internal terms

  - Abbreviations

It is also recommended to set the password expiration policy for the whole enterprise to ensure that passwords can't be hacked. See Figure 2-15.

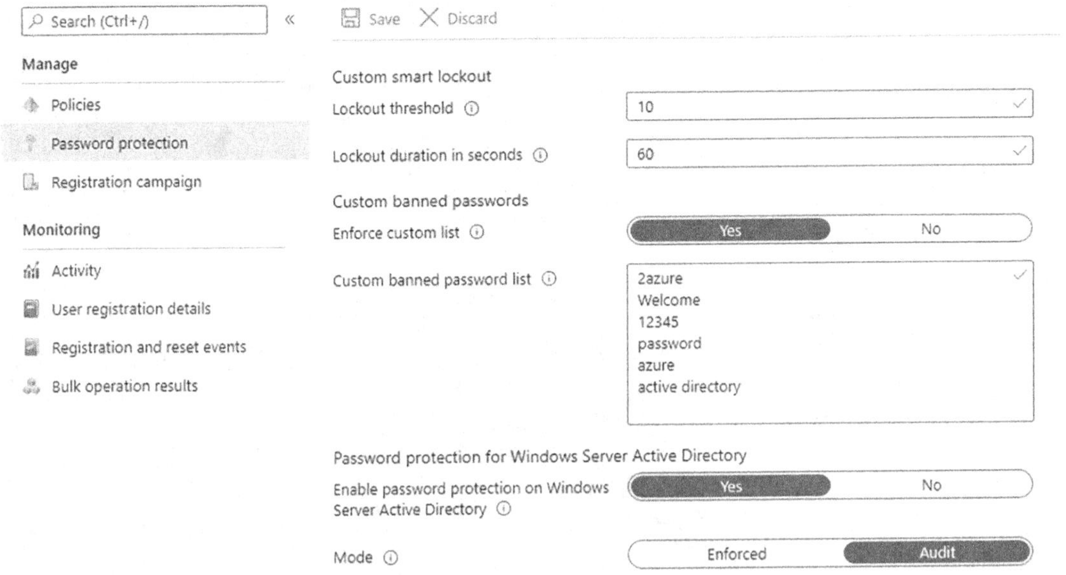

Figure 2-15. *Azure AD password expiration policy*

In order to set the password expiration policy, you need to sign in and access Microsoft 365 admin accounts. As an admin, you can set the passwords to expire after a certain number of days or never expire based on certain requirements. It is recommended to use multifactor authentication to secure these passwords. See Figure 2-16.

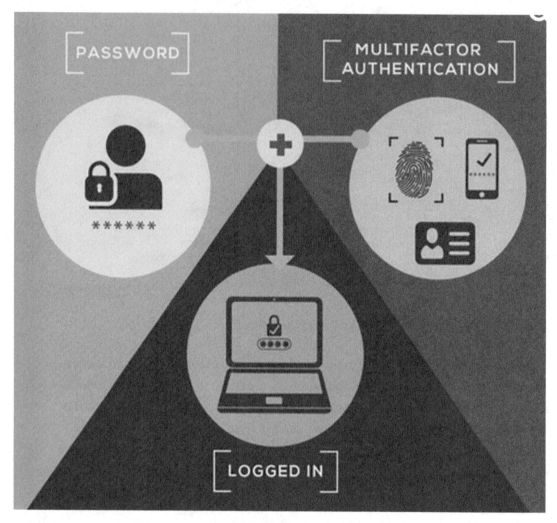

Figure 2-16. Multifactor authentication

Microsoft also provides recommendations for selecting passwords.

Resisting Common Attacks

This involves choosing whether users enter passwords from trusted devices and the length and uniqueness of the passwords. Figure 2-17 illustrates a brute force attack.

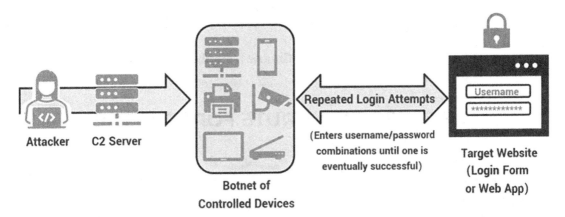

Figure 2-17. *Brute force attack*

- Restrict successful attacks: Resisting a hacker's attack is about restricting access to a specific service and limiting damage when the user password is stolen. For example, social networking credentials won't make your bank account vulnerable. Figure 2-18 shows some common cybersecurity attacks.

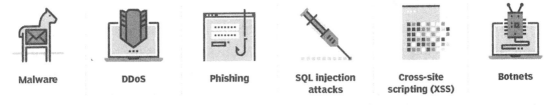

Figure 2-18. *Common cybersecurity attacks*

- Understand human nature: It is very important to understand human nature because the research shows that every rule set on the users will result in better password quality.

As an admin, you can set the password expiration policy to require strong passwords and minimize attacks:

1. Go to the Microsoft 365 Admin Center and click the Security and Privacy tab.

2. Select the password expiration policy.

3. If you don't allow users to set/change passwords, uncheck the box to Set Passwords to Never Expire.

4. Set the password expiration date. Choose a number of days from 14 to 730. See Figure 2-19.

KEY STEPS OF A BRUTE FORCE ATTACK

Attacker   **Guess List of Username & Password Combinations**   **Repeats Login Attempts Until One is Successful**   **Successful Credential Validation**

Figure 2-19. *Password expiration policy*

You can also sync user password hashes from the on-premises Active Directory to Azure AD. In order to synchronize the password, Azure AD extracts the password from the on-premises Azure Active Directory. Extra security processing has been applied to the password hash before it is synced with Azure Active Directory. See Figure 2-20.

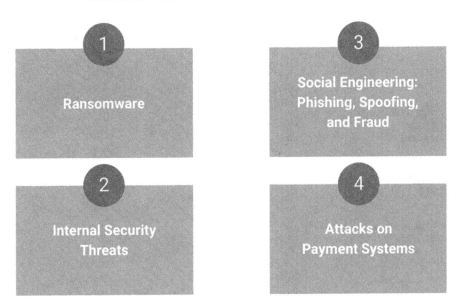

Figure 2-20. *Azure AD Password hash synchronization*

Active Directory Federation Services

Active Directory Federation Service is a simplified, secured identity federation. Federation mainly consists of a collection of domains with well-established trust between the entities. It can also include a collection of organizations that have established trust to share information and connections.

You can also federate the on-premises server or environment with Azure AD and use this federation with the authentication and authorization. Administrators can implement the access control federation with AD FS and PingFederate. See Figure 2-21.

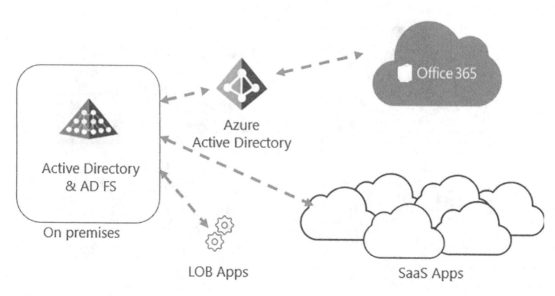

Figure 2-21. *Azure AD federation service*

Azure AD Connect enables you to configure federation with the on-premises Active Directory Federation service and Azure AD. Once you federate the on-premises server with Azure AD, all users on the on-premises server can use their on-premises user ID and password to log in and access the application or system. See Figure 2-22.

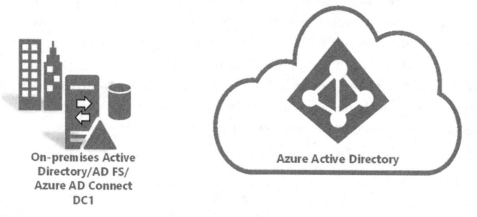

Figure 2-22. *On-premises Azure AD federation service*

Azure Active Directory allows you to configure federation with on-premises Active Directory Federation Service. Let's explore the various sign-in options for both cloud and on-premises resources:

- Password hash synchronization with seamless single sign-on (SSO)

- Passthrough authentication with seamless single sign-on (SSO)

- Federated SSO

- Federation with PingFederate

First you need to understand the authentication methods for the users to sign into Azure AD. Azure AD has various sign-in authentication methods:

- Cloud authentication: Azure AD handles the authentication process using the cloud to sign in to the application. There are two options for cloud authentication:

  - Password hash synchronization: Enables users to use the username and password that end users are using on the on-premises server without deploying any additional information. See Figure 2-23.

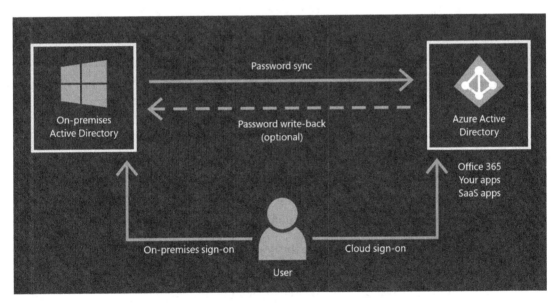

Figure 2-23. *Azure AD with password hash sync*

- Passthrough authentication: This option is similar to password hash sync, but it provides simple password validation using the on-premises software with strong security and compliance. See Figure 2-24.

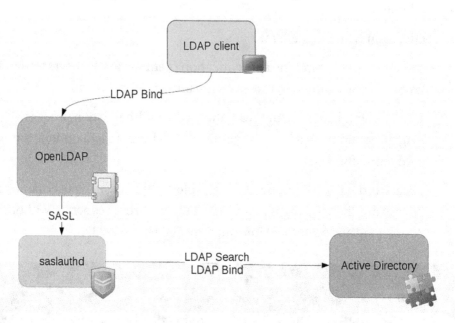

Figure 2-24. *Azure AD with passthrough authentication*

- As shown in Figure 2-24, with passthrough authentication, it will create a secure channel to Azure Active Directory. Once the secure channel is established, public and private keys are generated using Azure AD and then you can establish the connection to Azure SQL DB. Once the connection is established, certificates are issued.

- Federated authentication: With this federation authentication, you can hand over the authentication process to a separate, trusted authentication system, such as AD FS. See Figure 2-25.

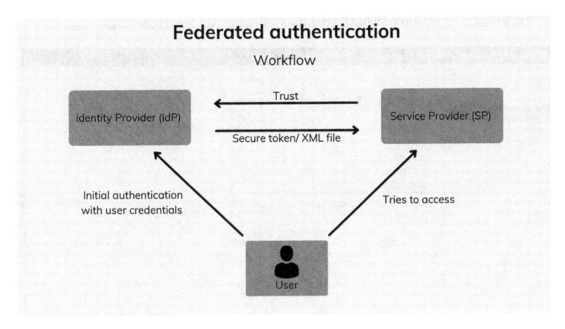

Figure 2-25. *Azure AD federated authentication*

You can change the sign-in method from the federation, password hash synchronization or from passthrough authentication using the tasks available in Azure AD Connect. Select Change User Sign-In from the tasks, as shown in Figure 2-26.

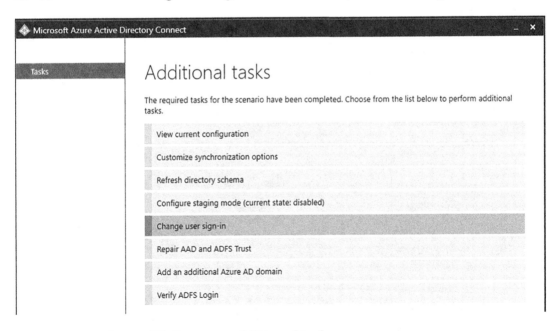

Figure 2-26. *Azure AD Connect additional tasks*

On the next page, you provide credentials for Azure AD. See Figure 2-27.

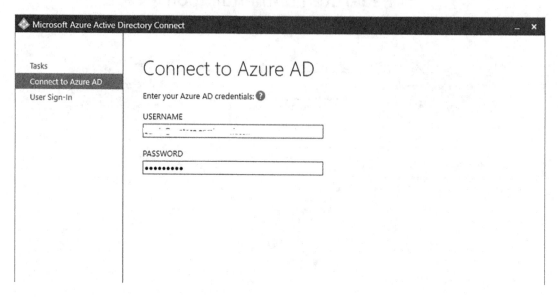

Figure 2-27. Connect to Azure AD

Now, from the user sign-in page, select the desired user sign-in. See Figure 2-28.

Figure 2-28.   *Connect to Azure AD*

Azure AD Application Proxy

Azure AD Application Proxy provides secure, remote access to on-premises web applications. Once they sign in to Azure AD, users can access cloud and on-premises applications using an external URL or an internal application portal. For example, once you set up Application Proxy, it can provide remote access and single-sign on to the remote desktop, SharePoint, Teams, Tableau, Qlik, and so on. See Figure 2-29.

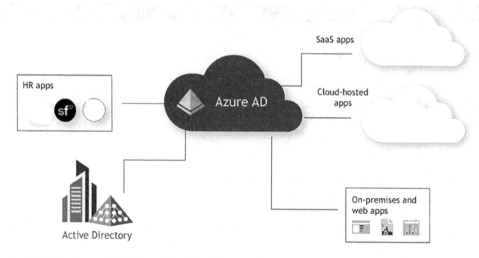

Figure 2-29. *Azure AD Application Proxy*

Consider these features of Azure AD Application Proxy:

- Simple to use: End users can access on-premises applications the same way using Microsoft 365 and other SaaS applications with Azure AD.

- Secure: On-premises applications can use Azure's authorization control and security analytics. For example, an on-premises application can use conditional access and two-step verification or multifactor authentication to make it more secure. Application Proxy doesn't require an open, inbound connection using the firewall.

- Cost-effective: You don't have to change the network infrastructure or install any additional software in order to use Azure AD Application Proxy.

Azure AD Application Proxy is a feature of Azure AD that accesses on-premises web applications from a remote desktop/client. It includes Application Proxy, which runs in the cloud, and the Application Proxy connector, which runs on the on-premises server.

Application Proxy works with the following:

- Access to the applications from the Remote Desktop Gateway

- Rich client apps with the Microsoft Authentication Library

- Web applications using header access

Application Proxy is recommended for giving remote users access to internal resources. It replaces the need for a VPN or reverse proxy and it is not needed by the internal users of the corporate world or an enterprise company.

Figure 2-29 shows Azure AD and Application Proxy working together to provide a single sign-on to on-premises applications.

First of all, the user has to access the application using the endpoint. The user is then directed to the Azure AD sign-in page. After the user successfully signs in, Azure AD sends the token to the user's client device. The client will then send the token to Application Proxy, which will retrieve the user's principal name and security principal name from the token. If the single sign-on is configured, the connector performs an additional authentication on behalf of the users. The connector then sends the request to the on-premises application and then the response is sent through the connector and Application Proxy service to the user. See Figure 2-30.

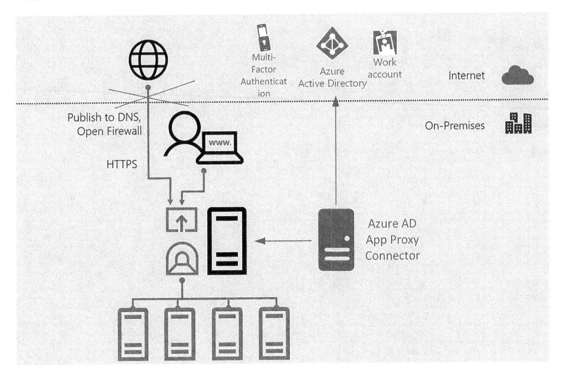

Figure 2-30. *Azure AD Application Proxy with conditional access*

Azure AD offers an Application Proxy feature that basically allows you to access your on-premises web applications using the remote client. It consists of two main components:

- Application Proxy Service: It runs in the cloud.

- Application Proxy Connector: It runs on the on-premises server.

This service and connector interact to securely transmit the user sign-on tokens from Azure AD to the web application.

The following are use cases for Application Proxy:

- It handles web application using Windows authentication for form-based access

- It supports applications protected by Remote Desktop Gateway

- It provides remote users with access to an internal resource without using the reverse proxy or virtual private network. Azure AD Application Proxy is only available with a premium license. See Figure 2-31.

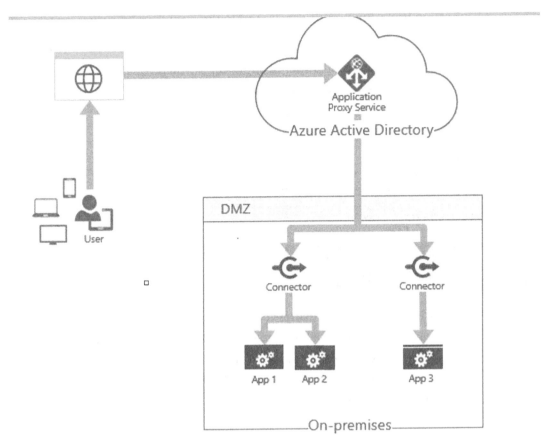

Figure 2-31. *Azure AD Application Proxy with on-premises*

The workflow of the Azure AD Application Proxy is as follows:

1. Once users have access to the application using the endpoint, Application Proxy directs them to the Active Directory sign-in page. When the conditional access policies are enabled, it will check for the conditions and comply with the security requirements.

2. If the sign-in is successful, Azure Active Directory will transfer the AD token to the client's device.

3. The client will then transfer the token to Application Proxy and access the token's security principal.

4. Application Proxy then sends the request to the Application Proxy connector.

5. Connectors then carry out authentication steps, which will then send the requests to the application's internal endpoint and forward the request to the application.

6. Connectors then forward the application's server response to Application Proxy.

7. Application Proxy then transfers the server's response to the user.

Exploring Azure AD B2B and B2C for External Partners

Azure AD B2B (Azure AD Business 2 Business collaboration) focuses on the problem of sharing applications with external users. These users can be suppliers, customers, or partners with whom you want to collaborate. You can invite external users to Azure AD to use your web application. You can also establish a connection between the ADFS server and the partner's application. See Figure 2-32.

Azure AD B2B

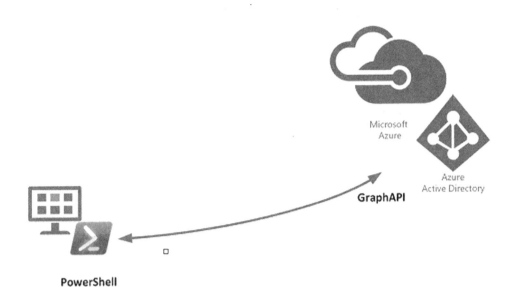

Figure 2-32. *Azure AD B2B*

You can invite Azure AD B2B users by email:

1. The end user will receive an email with the link to accept the invitation.

2. Authentication will happen at the right place once you click the link.

3. A trust relationship is established in the background without any configuration.

4. The entered credentials will be saved in a guest directory.

5. Access control is then managed in a host directory.

There are multiple ways to onboard users, depending on the relationship with the external users:

- Personal email invitation: Access packages (Individuals apply for access using an automated verification process.)

- Self-service user flows: Bulk invite via CSV upload.

Azure AD B2C (Azure AD business to customers) provides a security and authentication solution for external applications that are independent of your Azure AD. See Figure 2-33.

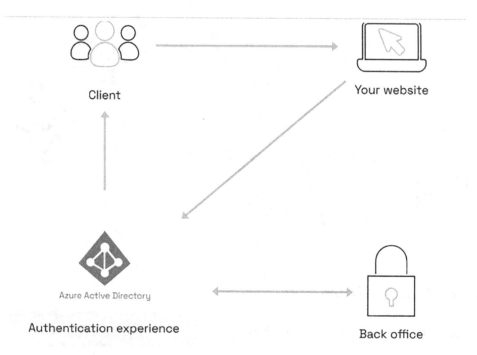

Figure 2-33. *Azure AD B2C*

The authentication process works the same way as with B2B, but it is not designed to work with internal users and employees, as it is mainly intended for end users. B2C provides complex user flows, such as policies. For example, existing customers with no relationship with the company need to be able to sign into the website and view documents. See Figure 2-34.

Figure 2-34. *Azure AD B2C flow*

To make this possible, Azure AD B2C needs to verify the customer's identity using an API call.

PIM Azure AD Identity Protection Hybrid Implementation

Privileged identity management (PIM) is a service of Azure Active Directory that helps users manage, control, and monitor access to resources within the organization. With PIM, you can secure resources in Azure AD, Azure, and other online services. See Figure 2-35.

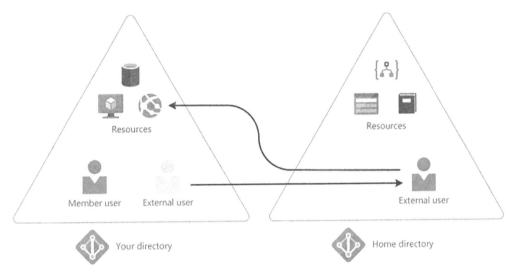

Figure 2-35. *Azure AD Privileged Identity Management*

Privileged Identity Management provides time-based and approval-based role activation to avoid the risk of unnecessary access permissions of resources. A few of its features are as follows:

- Enables just-in time access to Azure AD and resources
- Assigns timely access to resources using the start and end data
- Requires additional approval to activate the roles
- Uses multifactor authentication to activate the roles
- Conducts access reviews for user roles
- Exports the audit history for the internal and external audit

For Azure AD roles in privileged identity management, global administrators can manage the assignments for the other administrators. Azure resource roles can only be accessed by the subscription administrators, resource owners, or a resource user administrator. See Figure 2-36.

  Just-in-time and time-based access

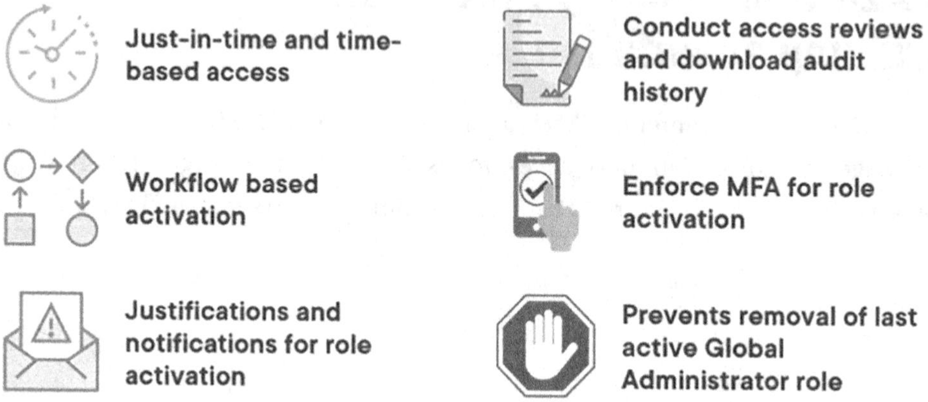

 Conduct access reviews and download audit history

 Workflow based activation

 Enforce MFA for role activation

Justifications and notifications for role activation

 Prevents removal of last active Global Administrator role

Figure 2-36. *Just-in time access*

Using Azure AD PIM, you can monitor, manage, and control access to your Azure resources. By reducing the number of people who have access, you prevent the following:

- Attackers or end users who perform brute force attacks on the entire system and find a way to steal information

- Unauthorized users being able to access data and resources by deleting, updating, or inserting data

Azure AD PIM can manage both Azure AD and Azure roles, and there is some overlap and differences between them. In addition to this, there are certain roles that can't be managed by Azure AD PIM. See Figure 2-37.

Roles that cannot be managed by Azure AD Privileged Identity Management

Account Administrator
Billing owner of the subscription, can create new subscriptions

Service Administrator
Manage services, cancel subscriptions, assign co-administrators

Co-Administrators
Similar to Service Administrator, assign users to co-administrator

Figure 2-37. *Azure AD PIM roles*

These roles can't be managed by Azure AD PIM.

- Account administrators

- Service administrators

- Co-administrators

With respect to Azure AD, there are two roles:

- Eligible roles: This is the type of role assignment where the end user needs to perform actions to activate and use the role. Once the actions are completed, the role types change from eligible to active. Once users are eligible for the role, they can activate the role using a privileged activity. See Figure 2-38.

My roles | Azure resources 📌 ⋯
Privileged Identity Management | My roles

《   ○ Refresh | ⌨ Got feedback?

Activate

🔹 Azure AD roles

👥 Privileged access groups (Preview)

🔹 Azure resources

Troubleshooting + Support

✖ Troubleshoot

📄 New support request

Eligible assignments   Active assignments   Expired assignments

🔍 Search by role or resource

Role	↑↓	Resource	↑↓	Resource type	↑↓	Membership	↑↓
				Resource group		Group	
				Resource group		Group	
				Resource group		Group	

Figure 2-38. *Azure AD privileged*

- Active roles: Role assignment that doesn't require users to perform an action using privileged roles. See Figure 2-39.

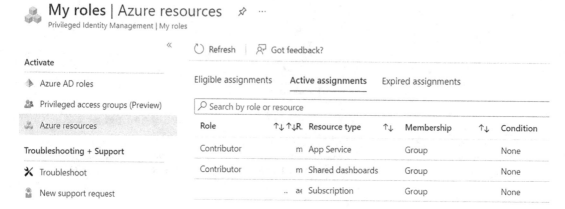

Figure 2-39. *Azure AD PIM active assignments*

Let's now look at the license requirements for users.

PIM Admin

The PIM Admin is the person who activates privileged identity management and provides consent. A global administrator does this task. They are the security administrator of the group that has authority to manage all the security aspects around Azure AD. See Figure 2-40.

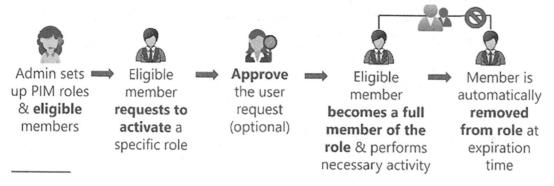

Figure 2-40. *Azure AD PIM admin*

Approvers

These are users who have the authority to approve or deny the role assignment requests using the PIM.

Access Reviewers

These users have been assigned the role to perform access reviews of the privileged role assignments to the users via PIM-eligible roles.

Single Sign-on with Azure AD

The Azure Active Directory single sign-on (SSO) feature allows users to sign in automatically when their corporate devices are connected to the enterprise corporate network. Once single sign-on is enabled for Azure AD, it allows users to sign in without entering their passwords and usernames.

Seamless SSO can be combined with password hash synchronization or passthrough authentication. You can't enable SSO with Azure Active Directory Federation. Enterprise organizations can protect sensitive data and applications, both on-premises and in the cloud, with integrated multifactor authentication. See Figure 2-41.

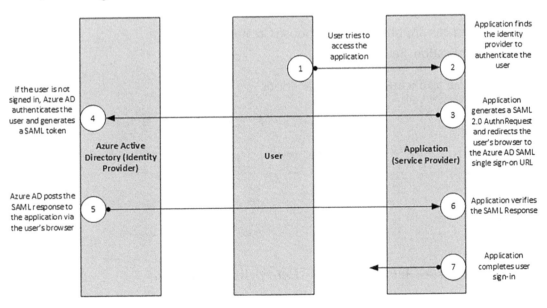

Figure 2-41. *Single sign-on SAML protocol*

SAML 2.0 sends authentication requests and responses to Azure AD using SSO. The cloud service uses HTTP redirection to pass the element to Azure AD. Azure AD then uses HTTP post binding to respond to the cloud service.

In order to configure SSO for Azure AD, you have to follow these steps:

1. Log in to the Microsoft Portal using the following URL: `https://portal.azure.com`.

2. Click the Azure Active Directory and select Manage Applications under the Manage tab. See Figure 2-42.

Figure 2-42. *Azure Active Directory*

3. Click New Application and choose Create the Enterprise Application. See Figure 2-43.

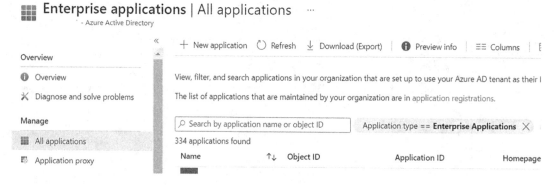

Figure 2-43. *Azure Active Directory - Enterprise Applications*

4. Open the enterprise application. From there, you can configure the application based on the required settings. See Figure 2-44.

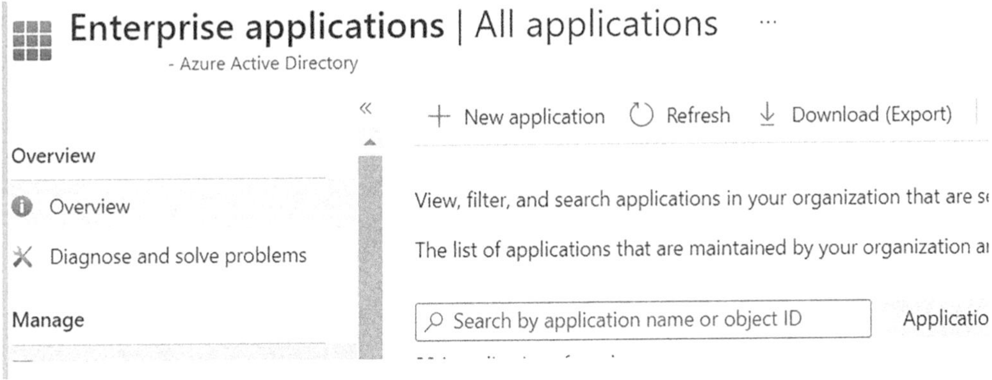

Figure 2-44. *Azure Active Directory - Create Enterprise Applications*

Conclusion

This chapter explored various identity protocols and their application types. You also learned about the Azure Active Directory security model and explored the Active Directory federation service and Azure AD Application Proxy, which is used to connect cloud applications with on-premises applications. You also learned about Azure AD B2B and B2C, which are for external partners using Azure AD. The chapter also quickly walked through the PIM implementation and its features using Azure AD and a hybrid implementation. In the end, you explored the single sign-on implementation using Azure AD.

CHAPTER 3

Network Security Patterns

Organizations typically focus on building applications and data-driven software to harvest value from thier data. An enterprise segmentation strategy helps technical teams create isolation across networks, applications, and identity-management systems.

The previous chapter explained how to set up Identity and Access Management (IAM) with Azure Active Directory (AAD).

This chapter covers the following topics:

- Software-defined networks (SDNs)
- Network topologies
- Segmenting subnets
- Controlling routing behavior
- Using gateways and firewalls

Software-Defined Networks (SDNs)

Software-defined networking is an architecture that's designed to centrally govern, manage, and configure virtual networking functionality with the help of software. Using SDNs, you can create cloud-based networks with routers, firewalls, and on-premises networks. See Figure 3-1.

© Sagar Lad 2023
S. Lad, *Azure Security For Critical Workloads*, https://doi.org/10.1007/978-1-4842-8936-5_3

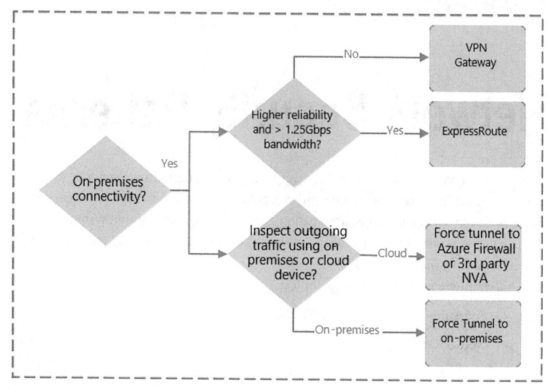

Figure 3-1. *Networking decision guide*

SDNs provide various options with differing prices and complexity. There are many ways to implement SDN technologies to create cloud-based virtual networks. Based on your governance requirements, you can structure the virtual networks for migration and interact with an existing IT infrastructure.

Types of virtual networking architectures:

- PaaS: All the PaaS products have limited built-in networking features. So, in most cases, you don't have to specify the software-defined network to support the workload requirements.

- Cloud-native: A cloud-native architecture supports cloud-based workloads using the virtual network that's built on top of the default software-defined networking capabilities. See Figure 3-2.

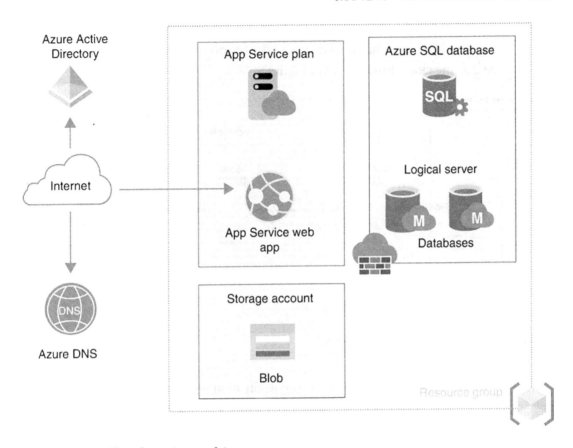

Figure 3-2. *Cloud-native architecture*

- Cloud Dematerialized Zone (DMZ): This cloud DMZ has limited connectivity between the on-premises and cloud networks, secured through a network implementation that controls the traffic between the environments. See Figure 3-3.

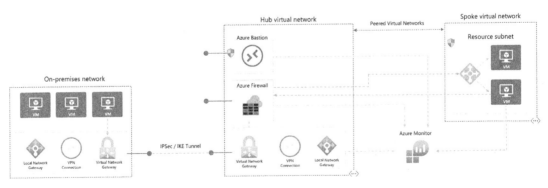

Figure 3-3. *Cloud DMZ*

- Hybrid: A hybrid cloud architecture allows virtual networks in the trusted cloud environments to access the on-premises resources as well as the cloud resources. See Figure 3-4.

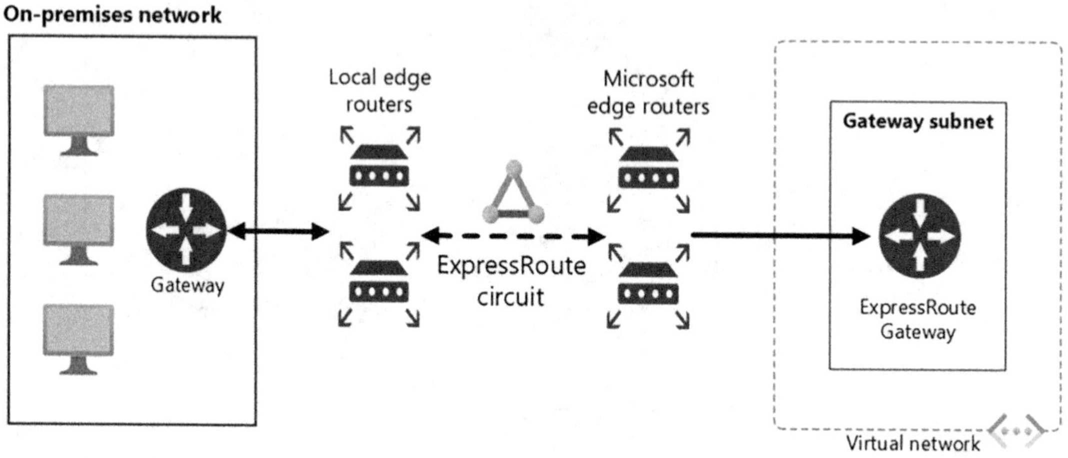

On-premises network

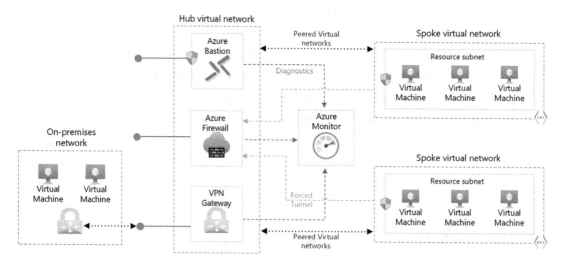

Figure 3-4. *Hybrid Virtual Network*

- Hub and spoke: This architecture centrally manages external connectivity and shared services to overcome potential subscription limits. See Figure 3-5.

Figure 3-5. *Hub and spoke model*

- Hub and spoke organizes Azure-based cloud network infrastructure into multiple connected virtual networks. The hub is a virtual network that acts as a central location to manage external connectivity. The spokes are virtual networks that host the workloads and connect to the central hub using *virtual network peering.*

Network Topologies

Network topology is the arrangement of a network consisting of nodes and how they connect to the sender and receiver. Let's look at the various topologies in detail.

Mesh Topology

In a mesh topology, every device is connected to another device using a specific channel. Mesh topology protocols used are AHCP (Ad Hoc Configuration Protocols) and DHCP (Dynamic Host Configuration Protocol). See Figure 3-6.

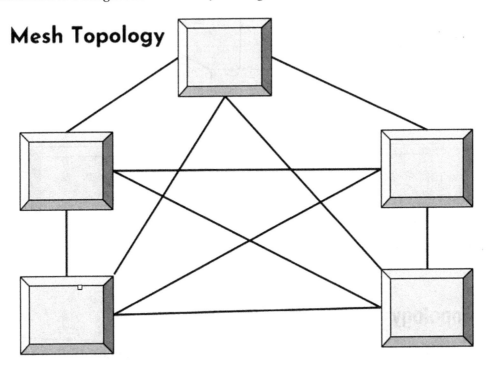

Figure 3-6. *Mesh topology*

Star Topology

In a star topology, all the devices are connected to a single hub using the cable. This hub is a central node and all other nodes are connected to it. Various popular protocols used in the star topology are as follows:

- Collision Detection (CD)

- Carrier Sense Multiple Access (CSMA)

One major problem with the star topology is that if the concentrator or connector fails, the whole system will crash. The cost of installing the star topology is also very high. The overall performance of the star topology is based on that single concentrator. See Figure 3-7.

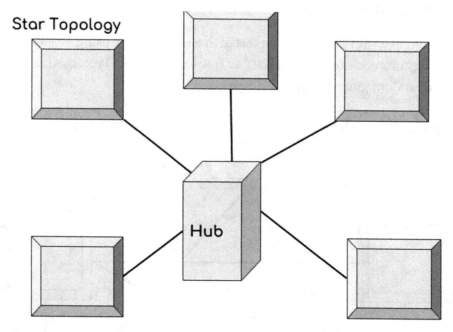

Figure 3-7. *Star topology*

Bus Topology

A bus topology is a type of network in which every computer and network device is connected to a single cable. A bus topology transmits data from one end to the other end in a single direction. See Figure 3-8.

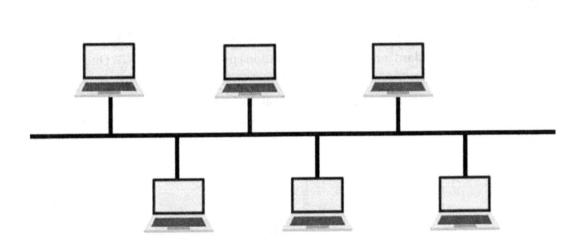

Figure 3-8. *Bus topology*

Ring Topology

This topology forms a ring by connecting a device to its two neighboring devices. In this topology, a number of repeaters are used with a large number of nodes. This is because, for example, if data has to be sent to 100 nodes, it has to pass through 99 nodes. This data transmission is unidirectional. See Figure 3-9.

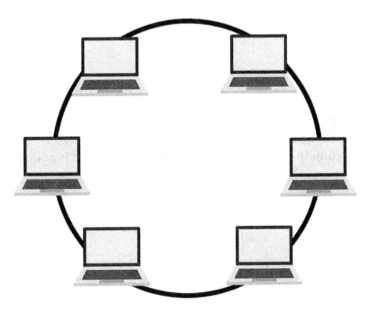

Figure 3-9. *Ring topology*

Tree Topology

Tree topology is a variation of star topology that has a hierarchical flow of data. This topology uses SAC (standard automatic configuration) protocols like DHCP. One major problem with the tree topology is that, if the central hub fails, the entire system fails and its cost is very high because of the cabling. It allows more devices to be attached to a single central hub. This way it decreases the distance travelled by the signal. See Figure 3-10.

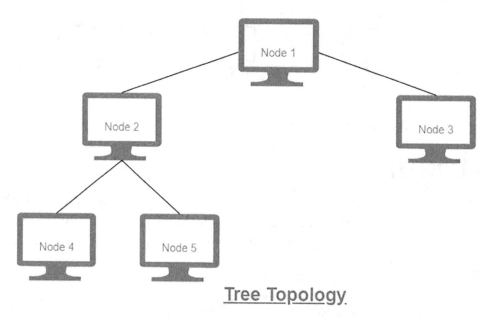

Figure 3-10. *Tree topology*

Hybrid Topology

A hybrid topology is a combination of various types of topologies. It is mainly used when the nodes are free to take any form. In a hybrid topology, each individual topology uses its specific protocol to get the work done. See Figure 3-11.

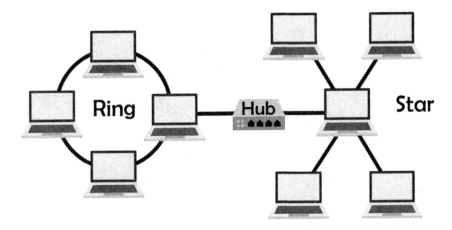

Figure 3-11. *Hybrid topology*

Segmenting Subnets

Enterprises need to create a strategy to consistently segment access to the application and data using the network, applications, and data and access controls. The main reasons for segmenting are as follows (see Figure 3-12):

- Group together similar assets that are part of the workload or application development

- Separate resources to improve security

- Set up and comply with governance policy as per the organization's standards

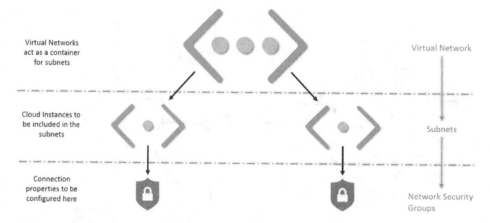

Figure 3-12. *Network segmentation*

With segmentation, you can create software-defined perimeters using various Azure services and features. When an application is placed in a separate segment, traffic between the segments will be controlled to secure the communication paths. The main advantage of segmentation is that, even if the segmentation is compromised, it will not affect the rest of the network.

When working with Azure, there are various segmentation options available:

- Azure subscription: Creates logical boundaries between the large teams/organizations within the company. This ensures that communication between the resources is provisioned explicitly. See Figure 3-13.

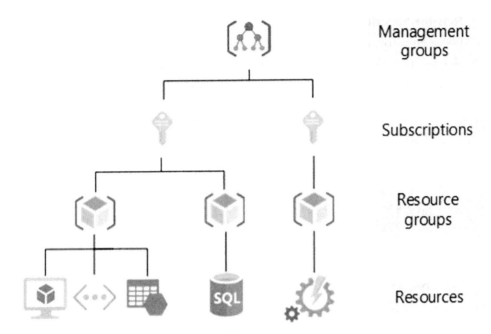

Figure 3-13. *Azure subscriptions*

- Virtual Network: Azure Virtual Network is a fundamental building block that creates a private network within the Azure environment. With VNET, you can enable many types of resources, such as Azure Virtual Machines, to securely communicate between the on-premises resources and any Internet resources. See Figure 3-14.

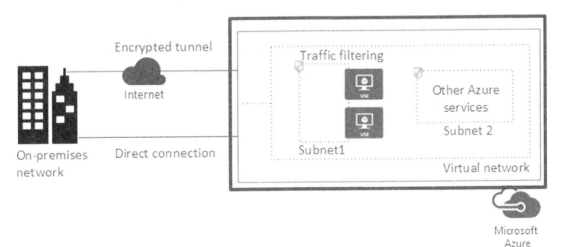

Figure 3-14. *Azure Virtual Network*

- Network Security Group(NSG): With NSGs, you can control traffic between resources within and outside the virtual network. You can also maintain granular access control by creating a separate logical environment for subnets, VMs, or group of VMs. See Figure 3-15.

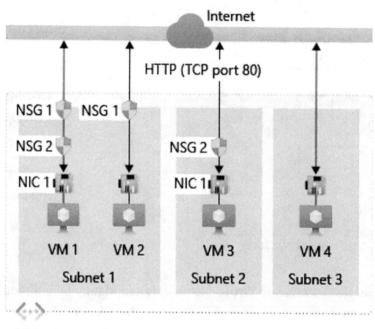

Figure 3-15. *Network security group*

- Application Security Group (ASG): Application Security Groups are the same as Network Security Groups, but they are referenced with respect to the application context. This allows groups of VMs under the application tag and defines the rules for each underlying VM. See Figure 3-16.

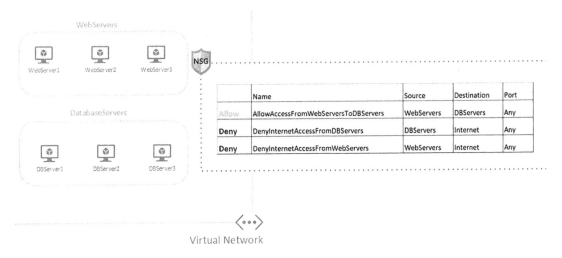

Figure 3-16. Application security group

- Azure Firewall: Azure has a cloud-native firewall that can be deployed to a virtual network or an Azure virtual WAN. It filters the traffic between the cloud resources, the Internet, and the on-premises server/resources. With Azure Firewall, you can create rules and policies and specify allow/deny traffic rules using layer 3 to layer 7 controls. You can also filter the traffic. See Figure 3-17.

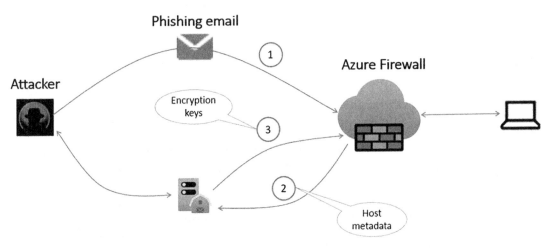

Figure 3-17. Azure Firewall

There are various standard segmentation patterns that isolate and secure workloads in Azure from a networking point of view. Let's explore these various standard patterns in detail and discuss which one is best from an organizational point of view.

- Single VNET: With a single VNET, all the application components reside in a single virtual network. When you are working in a single region and VNET can't span across multiple regions, you can use the single VNET approach. See Figure 3-18.

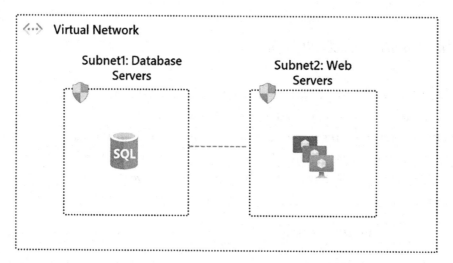

Figure 3-18. Single VNET

- Common ways to segment subnets or application groups include using the Network Security Groups and Application Security Groups. In Figure 3-18, Subnet 1 uses a SQL database and Subnet 2 uses Azure VMs. You can configure NSG to allow the communication between Subnet 1 and Subnet 2.

- Multiple VNET with VNET peering: Using the multiple VNET approach, you can spread resources across multiple VNETs. You can enable communication across the VNETs using VNET peering. VNET peering is recommended when you need to group applications in separate VNETs. When you use VNET peering, connecting between VNETs is not transitive. See Figure 3-19.

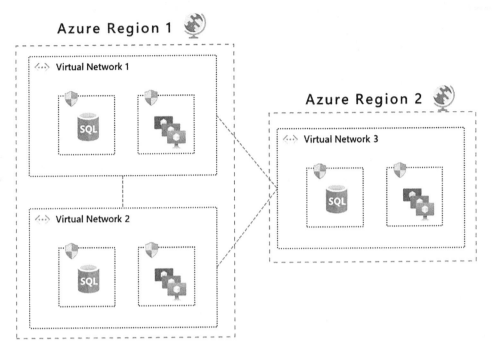

Figure 3-19. *Multiple VNETs with peering*

Controlling Routing Behavior

When you set up a virtual network for an application, you can determine the traffic between the services and within the virtual network by controlling the routing behavior. When you create a virtual network, you have default routes that will be enabled to allow that communication. In many cases, these default routes are sufficient to control the traffic within the VNET. If customization is required, you can customize the networking routes

Let's look at the concepts of routing the network traffic:

- System routes: Azure automatically creates a system route and assigns the routes to each subnet within a virtual network. Since these system routes are created by default, you can't create them and you don't have permission to remove them. But you can change or override the existing system routes using the custom routes. Azure creates default system routes for each subnet and it adds optional default routes to specific subnets using the Azure capabilities.

- Default routes: Each default route contains an address prefix and
  the next hop type. Whenever a virtual network is created, Azure
  automatically creates the default system routes listed in Table 3-1.

Table 3-1. *Default Routing Rules*

Source	Address prefixes	Next hop type
Default	Unique to the virtual network	Virtual network
Default	0.0.0.0/0	Internet
Default	10.0.0.0/8	None
Default	172.16.0.0/12	None
Default	192.168.0.0/16	None
Default	100.64.0.0/10	None

- Apart from the default routes, there are various other optional routes
  that can be configured. Depending on the capability, Azure adds
  optional default routes to specific subnets or to all subnets in the
  virtual network. See Table 3-2.

Table 3-2. *Optional Default Routes*

Source	Address prefixes
Default	Unique to the virtual network, for example: 10.1.0.0/16
Virtual network gateway	Prefixes advertised from on-premises via BGP, or configured in the local network gateway
Default	Multiple

- Custom routes: You can create custom routes either by creating user-defined routes or by exchanging the Border Gateway Protocol (BGP) between the on-premises network gateway and the Azure network gateway.

- User-defined routes: You can create user-defined routes in Azure to override Azure's default system routes or add more routes to the subnet's route table. You can create a route table and an associate route table to zero or more virtual network subnets.

- Border Gateway Protocol (BGP): On-premises network gateway can exchange routes with the cloud Azure network gateway using the Border Gateway Protocol. Using BGP with an Azure virtual network depends on the type of gateway. When you exchange routes with Azure using BGP, a separate route is added to the route table of all the subnets in the virtual network. See Figure 3-20.

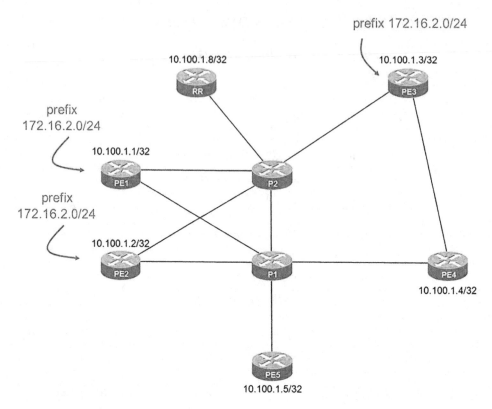

Figure 3-20. *Border Gateway Protocol*

VPN Gateway route propagation can be disabled on a subnet using the route table. Connectivity with VPN connection is achieved using the custom routes with the Virtual Network Gateway.

Using Gateways and Firewalls

In order to secure your Azure application workload, you have to make sure that all security measures—including authentication, authorization, and encryption—are properly in place. You can add security layers to the virtual machine where the application is hosted and deployed. These layers protect inbound flow from the users.

Azure Firewall is a next-generation firewall that provides network address translation. It is an intelligent firewall security and it provides the best of threat protection for the workload running in the cloud.

Azure Firewall standard provides L3-L7 filtering and threat intelligence directly from Microsoft Cyber Security. Azure Firewall Premium has advanced capabilities compared to Azure Firewall. These advanced capabilities include byte sequence in network traffic or attacks done by the antivirus or malware software.

You can properly govern and manage Azure Firewall across multiple subscriptions using the Azure Firewall Manager. With the Firewall Manager, you can apply the firewall policy to apply common network rules in the Azure AD Tenant. The Firewall Manager can support firewalls in both VNET and Virtual WANs. Azure Firewall is based on the five pillars of the architectural excellence:

- Reliability

- Security

- Cost optimization

- Operational excellence

- Performance excellence

Azure Application Gateway is a load balancer that helps you control and manage the traffic of web applications. With the application gateway, you can make routing decisions based on the HTTP requests.

With Azure Application Gateway, you can perform URL-based routing. You can enable Secure Socket Layer (SSL)/Transport Layer Security (TLS) gateways, auto-scaling, zone redundancy, static VIPs, and web application firewalls by enabling the application gateway.

Conclusion

This chapter explored in detail the software-defined networks and the approach to be followed by an enterprise organization. You also learned about various network topologies and how to use subnets in the virtual network to isolate the network traffic. You also learned that you can control and route traffic using the NSG rules and ASG.

CHAPTER 4

Infrastructure Security Patterns

Organizations typically focus on building applications and data-driven software to harvest value from their data. To create secure and reliable applications, setting up an infrastructure is a must. Security configurations must be done correctly in order to ensure that the applications function correctly, without any vulnerabilities or security concerns.

The previous chapter explored the infrastructure security patterns and discussed how to set up public cloud resources.

This chapter covers the following topics:

- Physical security

- Built-in Azure security controls

- Azure Tenant Security

- Container security

- Securing Azure resources

Physical Security

When you use public cloud platforms like Azure, the Microsoft Azure team has to secure the data centers and resources used in the background for the IaaS, PaaS, and SaaS services.

These data centers and resources should comply with industry standards to maintain the security and reliability of the application. Managing and maintaining these data centers and resources is handled by the Microsoft operations staff in the background, so customers can continue their work without the headaches of configuration, management, and maintenance.

© Sagar Lad 2023
S. Lad, *Azure Security For Critical Workloads*, https://doi.org/10.1007/978-1-4842-8936-5_4

Microsoft Azure has a globally distributed infrastructure that can support thousands of online services and secure facilities all over the world. There are a total of 58 regions and 140 countries worldwide. Microsoft Azure regions comprise an interconnected set of data centers via a massive network. This network includes distribution, load balancing, and encryption for ongoing traffic between the regions and outside the regions. Microsoft Azure has the largest number of regions across the world compared to other cloud providers. See Figure 4-1.

Figure 4-1. *Azure regions worldwide*

Azure regions are organized into geographies. This ensures that the data residency and the compliance requirements are honored with respect to the geography and the regions. These geographies are also fault tolerant, in case of any failures in the region, with dedicated infrastructure.

Each Azure region consists of availability zones. Availability zones are physical, separate locations within an Azure region. Each availability zone consists of multiple data centers with cooling, networking, and compute capabilities.

Figure 4-2 shows the overall global infrastructure with region pairs and availability zones within the data boundary for back up, disaster recovery, and high availability. This geographically distributed data center enables Microsoft to reduce network latency and backup failover.

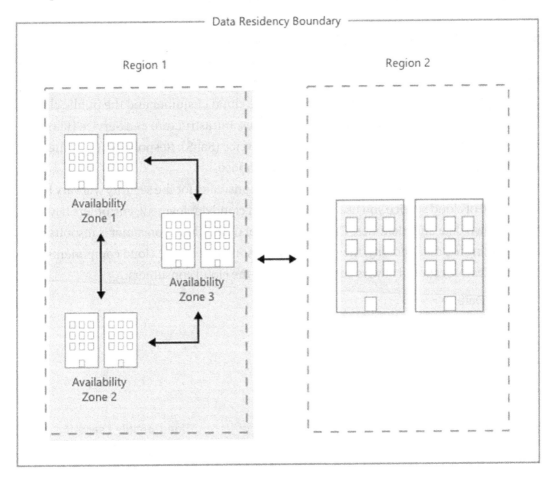

Figure 4-2. *Azure regions and availability zone*

- Physical security reviews: For a public cloud, you have to periodically perform a physical security review to address the Azure security requirements. End users don't have physical access to the Azure services and data centers where the Azure resources reside.

- Data bearing devices: Microsoft uses best practices and various industry standard procedures to handle the data-bearing devices. There might be various hard drives that can't be wiped.

- Compliance: The Microsoft Azure infrastructure also has a set of international compliance standards, such as ISO 27001,HIPAA, SOC 1, and SOC 2.

Let's explore in detail the built-in Azure security controls.

Built-in Azure Security Controls

While using a public cloud service, it is very important for enterprise organizations to know about the shared responsibility between the cloud customer and the public cloud offerings. Public clouds have three types of services: Infrastructure as a Service (IaaS), Platform as a Service (PaaS), and Software as a Service (SaaS). Responsibility for these services differs based on the type of service you choose.

Once you move the workload to the cloud, responsibility for the security will vary based on the type of cloud service you use. For any type of cloud deployment, customers have to use their own data and identities. The end customer or the cloud consumer is responsible for protecting the data security, the on-premises resources, and the cloud components. The following features should always be maintained by the cloud consumers:

- Data

- Endpoints

- Account

- Access management

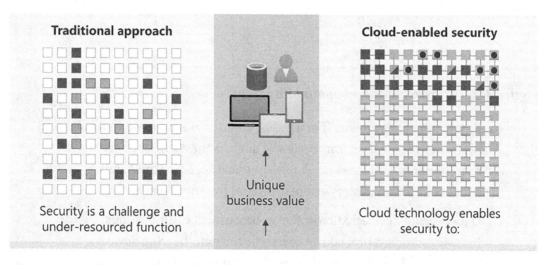

Figure 4-3. *Shared responsibility: traditional vs cloud*

Figure 4-3 shows the responsibility of the traditional application as well as the cloud application. One of the major reasons for using Azure cloud and its service is that it has a range of built-in security services and features that can be easily integrated to monitor the security features.

- Azure platform: With the Azure cloud platform, you can select from a range of operating systems, programming languages, frameworks, databases, and tools. See Figure 4-4.

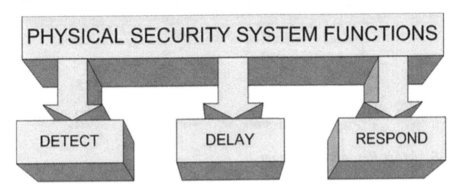

Figure 4-4. *Azure platform security*

Azure's public cloud infrastructure is designed to provide facility to applications to host millions of customers and provide a foundation when the security requirements are met. In addition to this, Azure also provides various security configurations so you can customize your security based on the needs and requirements.

- Azure Resource Manager: With Azure Resource Manager, you can work with resources to deploy, update, and delete all resources in the application. See Figure 4-5.

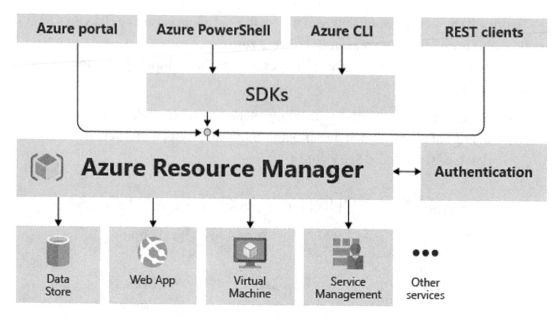

Figure 4-5. Azure Resource Manager

ARM Template deployment will work differently with different environments, such as development, testing, acceptance, and production. It provides security and auditing features so that you can manage resources after the deployment.

- Application Insight: With Application Insight, you can monitor applications when they are running as well as during testing and deployment. You can create charts and tables to find out more about how responsive the application is or to determine the overall performance of the application. See Figure 4-6.

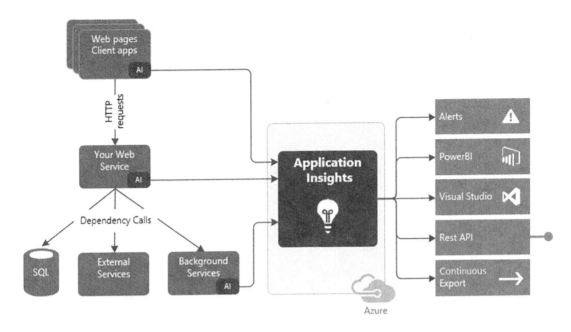

Figure 4-6. *Application Insight*

In case of any failures or performance issues, you can search through the logging data to determine the root cause.

- Azure Monitor Logs: These provide an IT management solution for on-premises as well as other cloud providers like AWS, Azure, and so on. They can be used to perform security as well as forensic logs. See Figure 4-7.

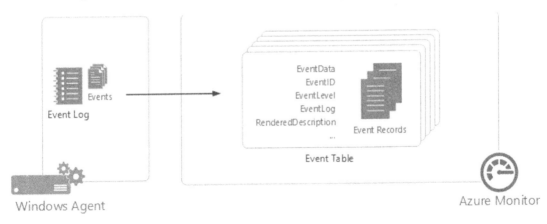

Figure 4-7. *Azure Monitor Logs*

- Azure Advisor: This is a personalized cloud service within Azure that's used to determine and optimize the security, cost, and performance of your cloud workload. Azure advisor uses configurations and telemetry to improve overall security, performance, reliability, and cost of applications as well services. See Figure 4-8.

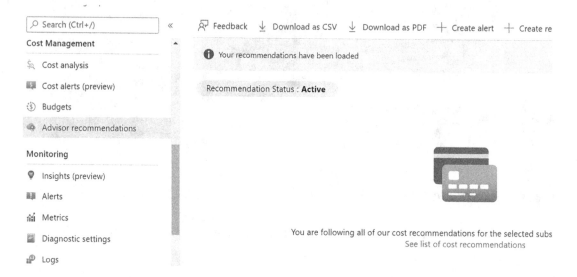

Figure 4-8. *Azure Advisor recommendations*

- As shown in Figure 4-9, you can look into the cost, security, reliability, and performance as well as operational excellence recommendations from Azure Advisor.

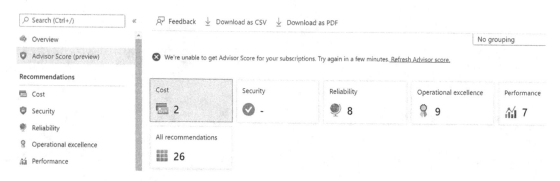

Figure 4-9. *Azure Advisor Recommendations categories*

From the left pane, you can select Security to learn more about the security recommendations in detail. With this feature, you can significantly improve the overall security of the application in Azure. See Figure 4-10.

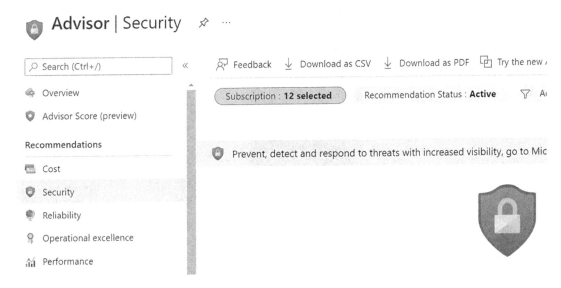

Figure 4-10. *Azure Advisor security recommendations*

- Web application firewall (WAF): With a web application firewall, you can protect your web applications from common attacks such as SQL injection, cross-site scripting (XSS), and session hijacking. It also helps enterprise organizations follow layered security approaches to make the application more secure and safe. Azure web application firewall on Azure application gateway provides protection from the web applications using the common security vulnerabilities. They target the attacks happening on the cloud resources and act based on the core rule set from the open web application security project. It operates as an application delivery control and provides a Transport Layer security layer, which was earlier known as the secure socket layer. This includes policy management and E2E TLS support. See Figure 4-11.

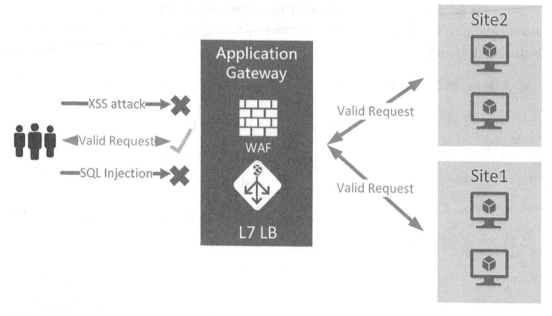

Figure 4-11. *Azure Web Application Firewall*

A layered security architecture incorporates the pros and cons of various security products. With layered security, you can put multiple security controls into the IT environment. A fundamental component of layered security is the perimeter of defense for traffic from the network. The Azure app service environment provides an isolated runtime environment that's deployed in the Azure Virtual Network. The major goal is to hide the API backends from Internet access. With Azure Virtual Network, you can also use Network Security Groups (NSGs) to allow or deny inbound or outbound traffic to and from the website and web application. You can also use private endpoints to restrict public access to the same.

Layered security refers to the multiple components to protect operations at multiple levels or layers. This security approach deploys multiple controls to protect sensitive areas of the technology where attackers can get access to the system or application. With a layered approach, you need to define the firewall, patch management, multifactor authentication, endpoint protection, and security awareness training to improve the overall security of the application. See Figure 4-12.

Figure 4-12. *Layered security architecture*

Let's now look at the Azure Tenant Security concepts.

Azure Tenant Security

Azure Tenant Security (AzTS) is a more scalable and robust solution. The Azure Tenant Security solution is based on the Azure functions and it is a central scan model where you can perform scanning using the managed identity. See Figure 4-13.

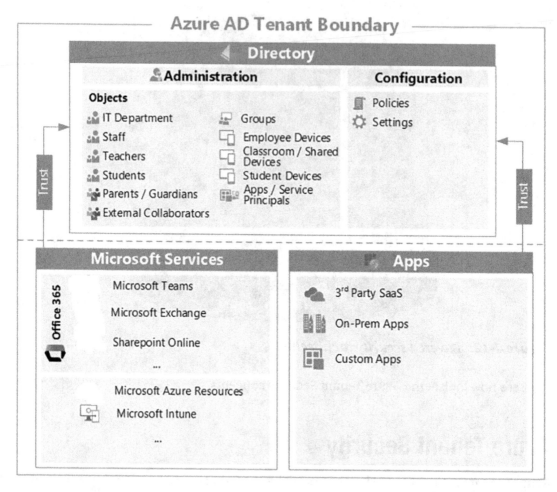

Figure 4-13. *Layered security architecture*

With the Azure Tenant Security solution, you can scale efficiently and use less overhead to get the same level of visibility. It is also designed to accelerate migration to Azure security offerings such as Policy, Security Center, Management Groups, and Azure Resource graphs. .

Now that you understand the basics of Azure Tenant Security, let's look at the step-by-step process for using Azure Tenant Security.

1. Download the PowerShell script from GitHub at:

   `https://github.com/azsk/AzTS-docs/blob/main/TemplateFiles/`
   `DeploymentFiles.zip?raw=1`

2. Open the folder in Windows Explorer and then open the
   `ExecutionScript.ps` file using the PowerShell IDE. See
   Figure 4-14.

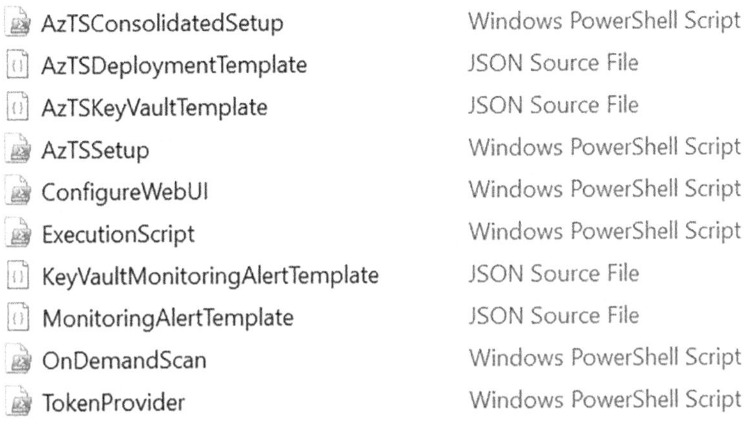

AzTSConsolidatedSetup	Windows PowerShell Script
AzTSDeploymentTemplate	JSON Source File
AzTSKeyVaultTemplate	JSON Source File
AzTSSetup	Windows PowerShell Script
ConfigureWebUI	Windows PowerShell Script
ExecutionScript	Windows PowerShell Script
KeyVaultMonitoringAlertTemplate	JSON Source File
MonitoringAlertTemplate	JSON Source File
OnDemandScan	Windows PowerShell Script
TokenProvider	Windows PowerShell Script

Figure 4-14. *Deployment script*

3. Now, change the information for `$TenantId`. You can get the
   information from the Azure Active Directory. See Figure 4-15.

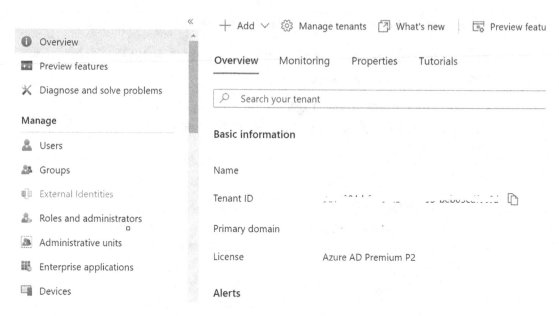

Figure 4-15. *Azure Active Directory*

4. Once the details are up to date, execute the script that will create
    the Azure services, as shown in Figure 4-16.

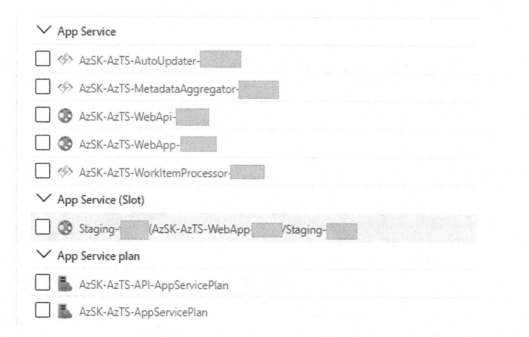

Figure 4-16. *Azure services*

5. Even though the services have been created, when you open the web app, the data is still blank. Be sure to execute this PowerShell command:

```
Start-AzSKTenantSecuritySolutionOnDemandSca -SubscriptionId
$HostSubscriptionId1 -ScanHostRGName $HostResourceGroupName1
```

6. Once that command is executed, it will open the web page shown in Figure 4-17.

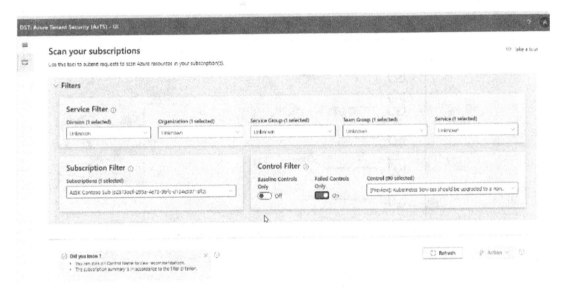

Figure 4-17. *Azure Tenant Security*

Azure Tenant Security can be used to obtain visibility of cloud subscriptions across multiple subscriptions in the organization. It is a DevOps kit that helps you move closer to the implementation of cloud security compliance on the Azure platform.

With Azure Tenant Security, you can perform the following activities:

- Scan multiple subscriptions with a central scan tool in a cheaper and more timely manner

- Auto-scale without any external constraints

- Speed up the effort of native features

- Enable incremental transition to the controls for custom code

Let's take a quick tour of container security.

Container Security

Considering the popularity and ease of setting up a Kubernetes cluster, many organizations use Kubernetes to orchestrate their containerized applications. Organizations need to consider and adopt Kubernetes security best practices for their containerized workloads. See Figure 4-18.

Figure 4-18. *K8 security checklist*

- Enable Kubernetes with role-based access control (RBAC): With RBAC, you can define permissions and determine who can access the Kubernetes API and related permissions at a granular level. Kubernetes combines the authorization controllers so it is better to disable the legacy attribute based access control. It is advisable to avoid granting cluster-level permission, even during troubleshooting. See Figure 4-19.

Role-Based Access Control

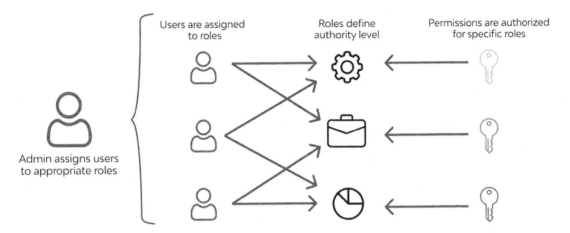

Figure 4-19. *Role-based access control*

- Keep Kubernetes up to date: As it is open source, Kubernetes has many contributors. Thus, it is important to stay up to date with the latest version, considering the security vulnerabilities and related updates.

- Integrate Kubernetes with third-party authentication: You can integrate Kubernetes with third-party tools, such as GitHub, for authentication. These tools provide additional security features like multifactor authentication, and so on.

- Limit direct access to the Kubernetes nodes: Limit SSH access to the Kubernetes nodes to avoid the risk of unauthorized access. You can also use Kubernetes authorized plugins to control user access to these resources.

- Set up administrative boundaries: You can create a Kubernetes namespace to partition the resources into logical groups. Resources created in one namespace won't be accessible to another namespace. You can even create policies to separate access between the namespaces.

For example:

```
        {
"apiVersion": "abac.authorization.kubernetes.io/v1beta1",

"kind": "Policy",

"spec": {

  "user": "sagar",

  "namespace": "cloud1",

  "resource": "pods",

  "readonly": true

        }
    }
```

- Enable network isolation: Running multiple applications on a Kubernetes cluster runs the risk of one application interfering with another. Therefore, network isolation is important to ensure containers can only communicate with appropriate containers. See Figure 4-20.

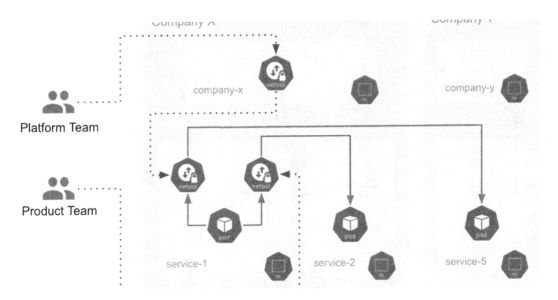

Figure 4-20. *K8 network isolation*

- Enable security context for pods and containers: While designing
  containers and pods, it is advised to configure the security context for
  the pods, containers, and volumes. You can define security context
  properties in the YAML format. See Figure 4-21.

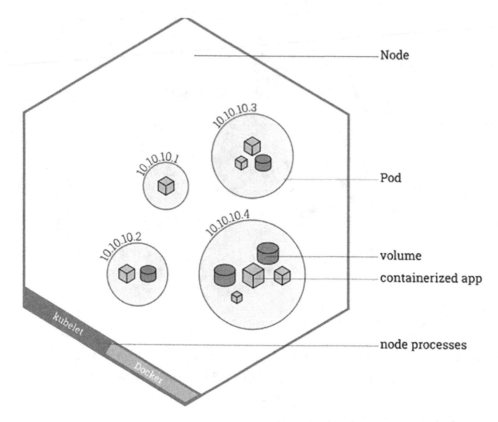

Figure 4-21. *Node, pod, volume and node process*

For example, pod definition with security context parameters:

```
apiVersion: v1
kind: Pod
metadata:
  name: first-pod-security-context
spec:
  containers:
  # specification of the pod's containers
  securityContext:
    readOnlyRootFilesystem: true
    runAsNonRoot: true
```

- Enable Kubernetes cluster logging: Enable logging for all cluster-related activities. You can also integrate the output of cluster logs with tools like Google Stackdriver logging or ElasticSearch.

- Secure secrets: Kubernetes cluster secrets contain sensitive information such as passwords, tokens, and SSH keys. Kubernetes supports encryption to ensure communication between the API servers is protected with TLS/SSL. It is also recommended to frequently rotate secrets to make it harder for attackers to gain unauthorized access to the cluster.

- Protect etcd with TLS, firewalls, and encryption: etcd stores the state of the cluster and confidential information in the form of secrets. It contains all the confidential information and is the highest-value target for attackers. If unauthorized users get access to etcd, the entire cluster is vulnerable to security attacks. See Figure 4-22.

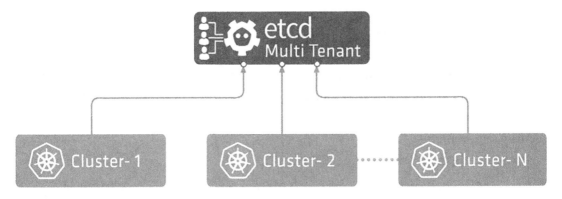

Figure 4-22. *etcd*

- Set up process whitelisting: Whitelisting is an effective way of identifying unexpected running processes. For this, you first need to understand the overall application behavior over a period of time. Then, use this pattern/list to whitelist the workload to the Kubernetes cluster. It is also difficult to do runtime analysis at the process level, but there are various solutions available in the market that minimize the overhead.

- Lock Kubelet: Kubelet is basically an agent that runs on each cluster node that interacts with the container runtime to launch the pods. Various configuration options are available to lock Kubelet to improve the overall security of the cluster.

- Disable anonymous access with `--anonymous-auth=false`: Unauthenticated requests won't be able to access the cluster and they will get an error response.

- Set `--authorization` mode: It is recommended to set the value for this variable to `AlwaysAllow` to verify that requests are authorized.

- Set `--read-only-port=0`: This configuration will enable read-only ports to prevent anonymous users from accessing information about running workloads.

Let's now look at how to secure Azure resources.

Securing Azure Resources

When you use a public cloud like Azure, deploying services and components is very easy and flexible. Before deploying the cloud application in the production environment, you have to make sure that the application follows the checklist for all the operational security requirements.

Consider this best practices checklist:

- Azure Role-Based Access Control (RBAC): Azure has various built-in roles to provide end users with the required permissions to the users, groups, or service principles. See Figure 4-23.

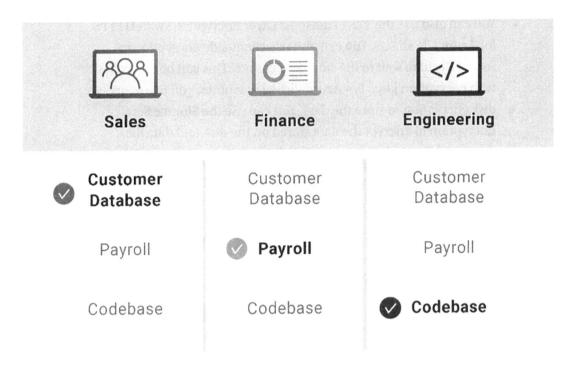

Figure 4-23. *Role-based access control*

- Data storage: In order to access and authenticate the data stored in the storage account, you can use the shared access signature (SAS). See Figure 4-24.

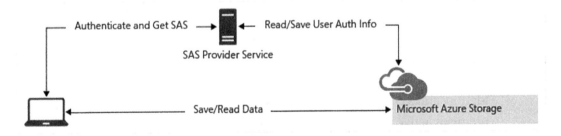

Figure 4-24. *Data storage*

- You can also use the TLS (Transport Layer Encryption) with HTTPS for Azure File shares. You can also use client-side encryption to secure the data sent to the storage accounts. This can be controlled with encryption keys. For Azure Virtual machines, you use Azure disk encryption to store the data. You can use the Storage Service Encryption to encrypt the data stored on the disk and data files.

- Using the Azure storage analytics, we can monitor the authorization type based on the storage account keys or shared access signature. See Figure 4-25.

SSE+CMK Workflow

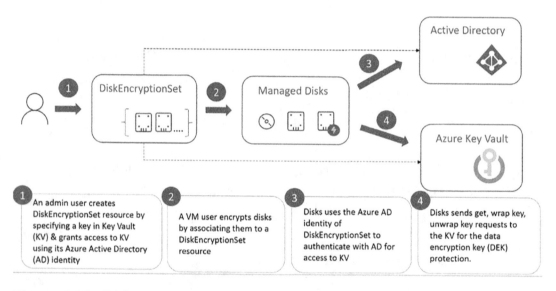

Figure 4-25. *Disk Encryption with SSE*

- Identity and Access Management: The first step is to sync your on-premises active directory with Azure Active Directory. You can also use single sign-on to enable access to the SaaS applications based on the accounts in Azure. You can also enable multifactor authentication for users to make authentication and authorization more secure. Using Azure AD premium, you can actively monitor suspicious activities. See Figure 4-26.

- Instead of using personal accounts, developers can use applications like Microsoft software development lifecycle.

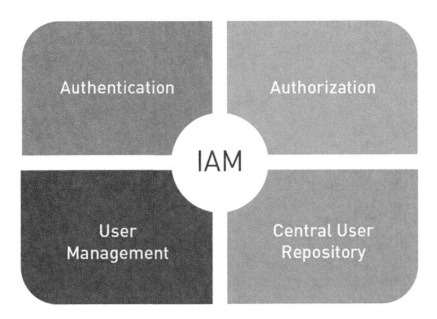

Figure 4-26. *Identity and access management*

Conclusion

This chapter explored how cloud providers use and manage public security of their infrastructure. In addition to this, you also took an in-depth tour of the built-in security controls available on the Microsoft Azure cloud. You also learned about Azure Tenant Security, with a step-by-step guide, and learned how to follow best practices to improve container security. Finally, you explored the security controls available in Azure's services and resources.

CHAPTER 5

Application and Data Security Patterns

Organizations typically focus on building applications and data-driven software to harvest value from their data. Application security mainly attempts to prevent data or code from being stolen. Application security considerations include hardware, software, and procedures to minimize security vulnerabilities.

The previous chapter explored how to set up your cloud infrastructure and strategies to make it secure.

This chapter covers the following topics:

- Securing application access

- Data classification

- Securing data access

- Data encryption patterns

Securing Application Access

In traditional application development and environments, securing data and software applications involves the on-premise network perimeter and physical access to the data. Considering the current trend where software developers are able to work from home using the Bring Your Own Device (BYOD) concept and mobile and cloud applications, most of the workload happens outside the company's network.

Identity is considered the new security boundary for the enterprise organizations. So, providing a granular level of access and enabling only valid users to access the system is the key to controlling your data and applications.

111

© Sagar Lad 2023
S. Lad, *Azure Security For Critical Workloads*, https://doi.org/10.1007/978-1-4842-8936-5_5

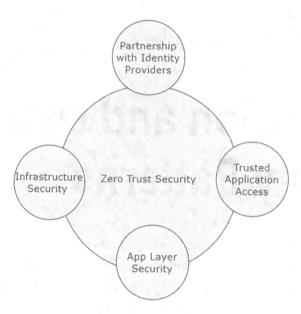

Figure 5-1. *Zero trust cloud security*

With zero trust cloud security (see Figure 5-1), cloud applications securely connect users to the applications. Authentication and authorization are required during the resource access in cloud infrastructure.

- The layered security approach with defense-in-depth: With layered security, you can easily detect attempts to access unauthorized access to the data. Since there are multiple layers, if one layer is breached, another layer is in place to prevent exposure.

- Regarding the PaaS and SaaS components of Microsoft Azure, Microsoft has a layered approach to security for physical data centers as well as across all Azure services. It protects information from intruders and prevents the data/information from being stolen.

- Confidentiality: Only authorized users can access the application. With the principle of least privilege, an entity or ID should be given only those privileges that are absolutely required to complete its tasks. Only individuals or non-personal entities who have explicit access can use the application. This includes securing user passwords, email content, or certificates.

- Integrity: In order to achieve integrity of an application, the goal is to prevent unauthorized changes to the data/information while the data is in rest or in transit. The standard approach while sharing data is that the sender creates unique fingerprint data using the hashing algorithm. The hash is then sent to the receiver along with the data. The receiver then checks the integrity of the data by calculating and comparing the hash to see if any data was lost or changed in transit.

- Availability: Cloud providers need to make sure that all services are available to authorized users. Denial of service attacks are the major reason to make applications unavailable to end users. Another major reason for the non-availability of the application is due to the natural disasters.

Now that you've read about the basics of application security, let's look at the security layers. You can think of layered security as a set of concentric rings, with the data being at the center, and it should be secured.

- Data: In a cloud environment, data normally resides as follows:

  1. Database

  2. Virtual machine disk

  3. SaaS application such as Microsoft 365

  4. Cloud storage

- Applications: You need to make sure that your applications are secure and free of vulnerabilities. Sensitive information should be stored in a secure storage mechanism. Integrating security into the application development lifecycle will lessen security vulnerabilities in the code. See Figure 5-2.

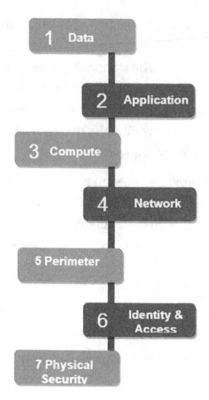

Figure 5-2. *Security layers*

- Compute: All compute resources should be kept secure by making sure that malware and patches are applied on time.

- Networking: Resource communication should be limited by using segmentation and access control. Inbound and outbound traffic should be denied by default and limited traffic should be open based on requirements.

- Perimeter: In order to avoid denial of service for end users, you can use the distributed denial of service (DDoS) protection. You can also use the perimeter firewalls to identify and alert about attacks against the network.

- Identity and access: The main goal of this security layer is to make sure that identities are secure and use a single sign-on and multifactor authentication for login and access management.

- Physical security: Physical security of the building and controlled access to the computer hardware in the data center is a top-most priority above all security layers.

Now that you have an understanding of application security access, the next section covers identity management in detail.

Identity Management

Digital identities are an integral part of enterprise organizations working on cloud or on-premise. Earlier identity and access services were restricted to operate only within the company's internal environment, so protocols like LDAP and Kerberos were designed and implemented.

Nowadays, mobile devices have become a primary way to interact with digital services. Organizations must evaluate the capabilities of the architecture in terms of its ability to bring such capabilities into the applications.

- Single sign-on: In a normal scenario, users have to manage multiple usernames and passwords to access applications/systems or services. More identities mean more usernames and passwords to remember. It becomes difficult for users to remember all that information. With single sign-on, users need to remember only one user Id and password. Access across the application is granted to one entity, which simplifies the security model. You can use Azure AD to enable single sign-on, which has a capability to combine multiple data sources into the security graph.

- Multifactor authentication (MFA): With multifactor authentication, you can add a layer of security to the application by requiring two or more elements for full authentication. Multifactor authentication enables security this way:

  - Something you know (for example, password)

  - Something you have (for example, security token)

  - Something you are (for example, biometrics such as fingerprints or face recognition)

- It increases the security of the identity by limiting the impact of confidential information being leaked. Azure AD has built-in multifactor authentication capability. Basic authentication features are available to Microsoft 365 and Azure AD administrators at no cost.

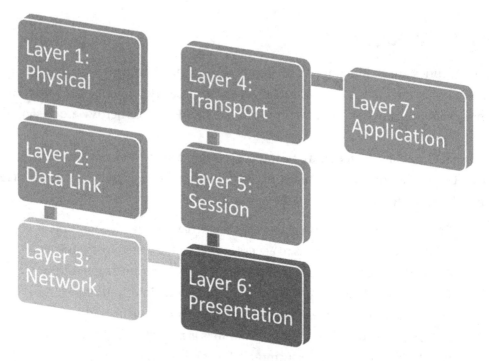

Figure 5-3. *Azure AD multifactor authentication*

The next section takes a quick tour of data classification.

Data Classification

Data classification sorts data to determine and assign value to it. It categorizes the data by sensitivity and business impact to identify the risks. Since the data is classified, you can manage the data to protect the sensitive information from loss. It is a process of linking metadata with every asset in a digital estate, which identifies the type of data.

The following are ways to classify data as per the Microsoft standard. Depending on your needs or security requirements, data classification standards may already exist in your organization. If no standard exists, you can use the following sample classification:

- Non-business: Personal data that doesn't belong to the organization

- Public: Data that is freely available and approved for public use

- General: Data that is available but not approved for public use

- Confidential: Data that can create issues if it is shared with other people

- Highly confidential: Business data that can create major issues for an organization if it is overshared

Microsoft Azure SQL DB has a built-in data discovery and classification feature that provides basic capabilities to discover, classify, label, and report sensitive data in an Azure SQL database. Sensitive data often consists of personal or financial information. Azure SQL DB can be considered a platform to fulfil the following data classification requirements:

- Achieve standards of data privacy and audit regulatory compliance

- Access sensitive data in a controlled manner and audit data access for security purposes

- Harden the security database that contains sensitive data

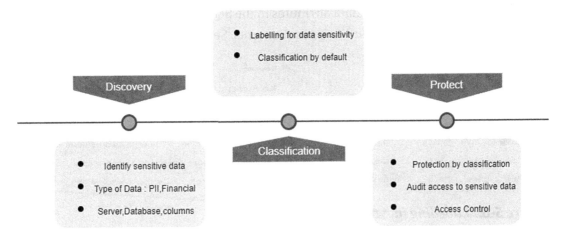

Figure 5-4. *Data discovery and classification*

Data discovery and classification (see Figure 5-4) supports the following capabilities in Azure SQL Database:

- Discovery and recommendations: A classification engine scans the database and detects the columns in the database that might contain personal sensitive information. Based on the data, it provides a recommendation to review and apply classification using the Azure Portal. See Figure 5-5.

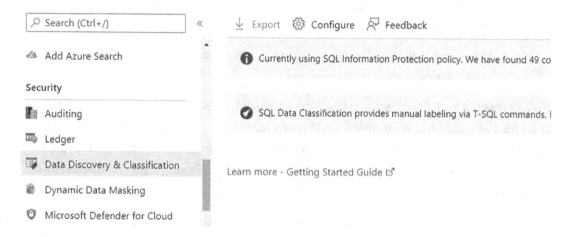

Figure 5-5. *Data discovery and classification in Azure SQL DB*

- Labels: Using this feature, you can apply labels to the columns based on the metadata attribute available in the SQL database. You can take into account the metadata attributes in the SQL database based on the compliance and auditing requirements. See Figure 5-6.

Display name	State	Description
Public	Enabled	Business data that is specifically prepared and approved for public consumption
General	Enabled	Business data that is not intended for public consumption. However, this can be
Confidential	Enabled	Sensitive business data that could cause damage to the business if shared with u
Confidential - GDPR	Enabled	Sensitive data containing personal information associated with an individual, tha
Highly Confidential	Enabled	Very sensitive business data that would cause damage to the business if it was sl
Highly Confidential - GDPR	Enabled	Sensitive data containing personal information associated with an individual, tha

Figure 5-6. *Labelling in Azure SQL DB*

- Query execution sensitivity: Once you execute the query, sensitivity of the query result is determined for auditing purposes.

- Dashboards: The SQL user can view the classification of the underlying data in visualized dashboards. You can also download reports in Excel format for auditing and governance purposes. See Figure 5-7.

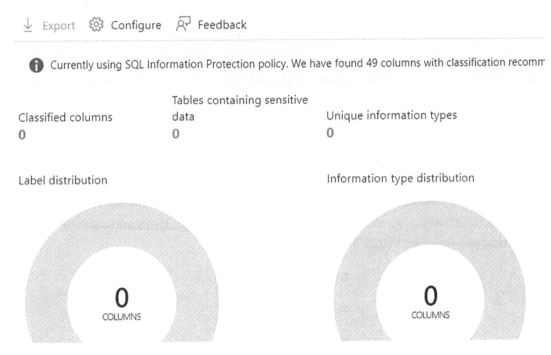

Figure 5-7. Azure SQL DB data classification dashboards

- Azure SQL offers the SQL Information Protection Policy as well as the Microsoft Information Protection policy to classify data. You can use either of them to discover and classify your data.

- SQL Information Protection Policy: Data discovery and classification has an built-in feature of sensitivity labels and information types that have discovery logic. You can define and customize the classification inside the central place using the Azure organizations. This central place is the Microsoft defender from the security policy. Only administrators of the management group can execute this activity. See Figure 5-8.

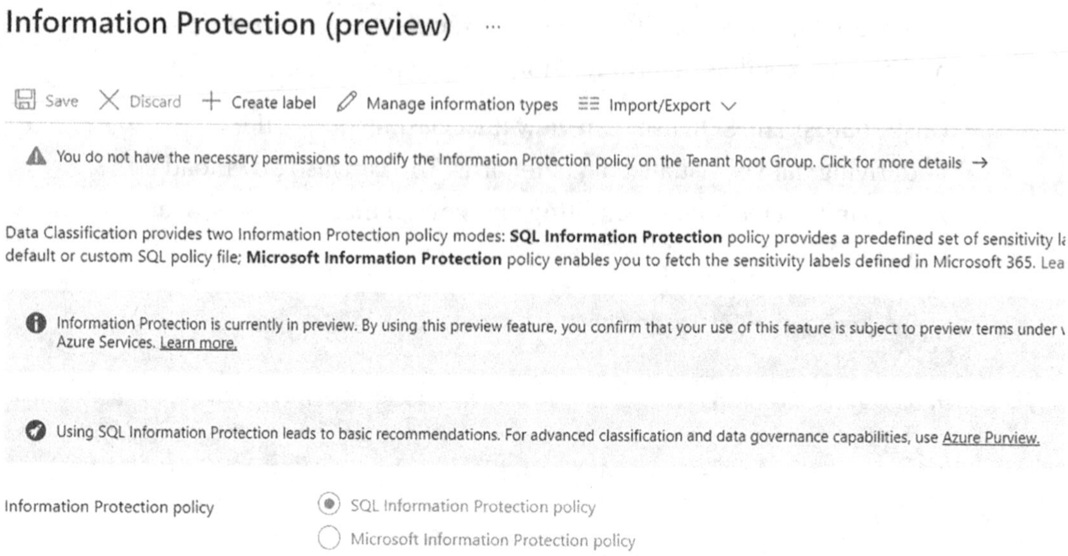

Information Protection (preview)   ...

🖫 Save   ✕ Discard   + Create label   ✎ Manage information types   ☰ Import/Export ⌄

⚠ You do not have the necessary permissions to modify the Information Protection policy on the Tenant Root Group. Click for more details →

Data Classification provides two Information Protection policy modes: **SQL Information Protection** policy provides a predefined set of sensitivity la default or custom SQL policy file; **Microsoft Information Protection** policy enables you to fetch the sensitivity labels defined in Microsoft 365. Lea

ⓘ Information Protection is currently in preview. By using this preview feature, you confirm that your use of this feature is subject to preview terms under \
Azure Services. Learn more.

✅ Using SQL Information Protection leads to basic recommendations. For advanced classification and data governance capabilities, use Azure Purview.

Information Protection policy   ⦿ SQL Information Protection policy
                                       ◯ Microsoft Information Protection policy

Figure 5-8. *Azure SQL DB Information Protection*

During policy management, you can define custom labels, rank them, and associate them with information types. You can add custom information types and configure them with string patterns. See Figure 5-9.

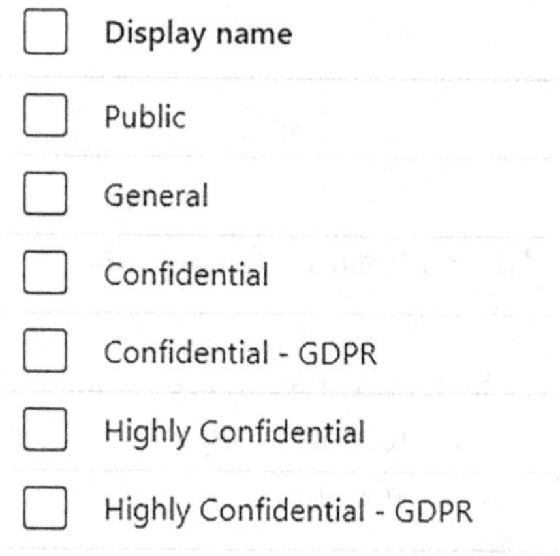

☐ **Display name**

☐ Public

☐ General

☐ Confidential

☐ Confidential - GDPR

☐ Highly Confidential

☐ Highly Confidential - GDPR

Figure 5-9. *Azure SQL DB Information Protection Policy Labels*

If you want to classify your database using the SQL information protection policy mode, follow these steps:

1. First go to the Azure Portal using the link: `https://portal.azure.com/`

2. Go to the Azure database and open the Data Discovery and Classification option from the Security section. The Overview tab has a summary of classification from the SQL database.

3. It also has an option to download the report in Excel. Click the Export button in the top pane to do this. See Figure 5-10.

Information Protection (preview)   ...

Figure 5-10. *Azure SQL DB Data Discovery an Classification: Export option*

4. In order to classify your data, select the Classification tab from the Data Discovery and Classification page. This classification engine scans the data and identifies any columns that contain personal and sensitive information.

5. Next, apply the classification recommendations as follows. First select the recommendation panel from the bottom pane.

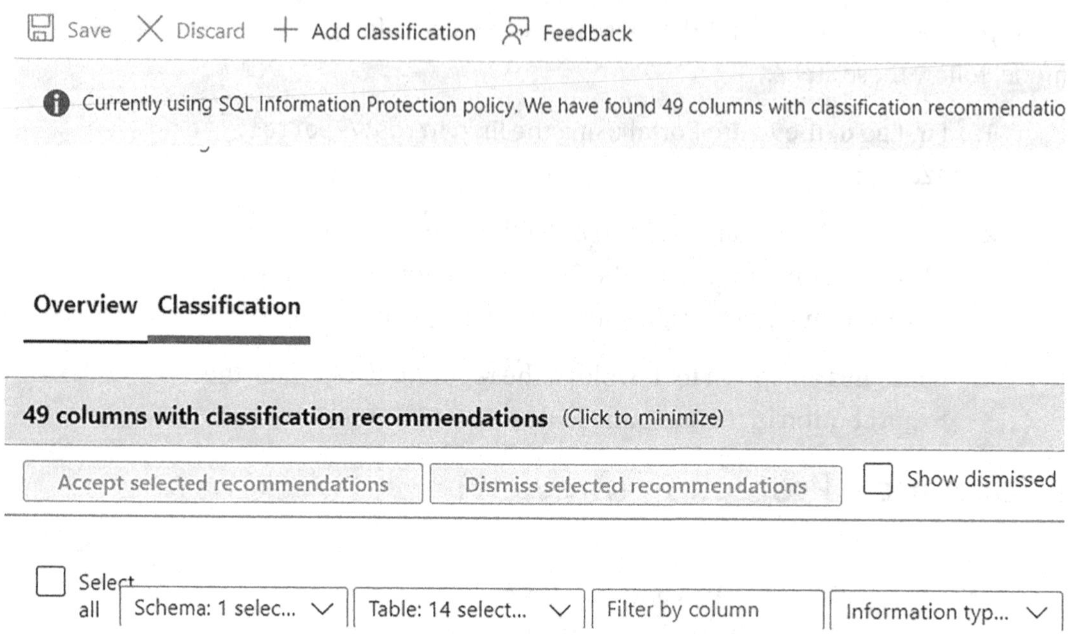

🖫 Save   ✕ Discard   + Add classification   🗩 Feedback

ⓘ Currently using SQL Information Protection policy. We have found 49 columns with classification recommendatio

Overview   Classification

49 columns with classification recommendations (Click to minimize)

| Accept selected recommendations | Dismiss selected recommendations | ☐ Show dismissed |

☐ Select all | Schema: 1 selec... ∨ | Table: 14 select... ∨ | Filter by column | Information typ... ∨ |

Figure 5-11. *Azure SQL DB classification recommendations*

You can accept the recommendations for a specific column or ignore them based on your choices. In order to apply the recommendations, choose the Accept Selected Recommendations option.

On the other hand, Microsoft Information Policy labels provide a simple way for end users to classify sensitive data across various Microsoft applications. These sensitivity labels are created and maintained in the Microsoft 365 compliance center.

Let's now go through the process of securing data access.

Securing Data Access

Public cloud services offer various in-built features to secure access to the data stored in cloud storage services. Configuring these features enables enterprise organizations to secure and protect sensitive information. However, many companies fail to protect their data due to misconfigurations or lack of awareness. Securing data is not only the responsibility of cloud providers but it is also the responsibility of enterprise organizations to properly configure security settings. See Figure 5-12.

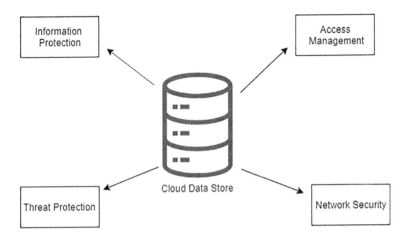

Figure 5-12. *Cloud data security*

Major challenges faced by enterprise organizations to secure and monitor data usage are as follows:

- Centrally monitoring security events in the logs

- Encrypting data at rest and in transit

- Guaranteeing authenticated and authorized access to data

- Handling centralized identity management for securely accessing stored data

Data Protection

The first step to protecting information is to identify and determine which data should be protected and where it resides. There are three types of data: data at rest, data in transit, and data that's in use (see Figure 5-13). Once you identify the location, the next step is to create clear, simple guidelines to secure the data. Once the data is available in the cloud storage, you need to protect the data at rest and in transit.

- Data at rest: You need to protect the data that exists statically or physically inside the cloud storage.

- Data in transit: When data is being transferred to components or locations over the network or across the service bus, it must be secured.

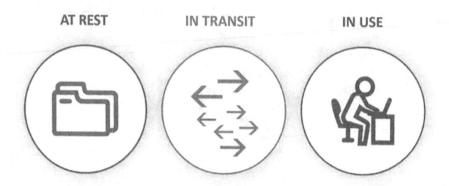

Figure 5-13. *Data at rest or in transit*

Access Control

Securing and administrating data stored in the cloud is a combination of identity access management and control.

Here is the communication flow for single sign-on (SSO) implementation.

- Centralized identity management. Centralized identity management enables much easier authentication and authorization to manage enterprise applications.

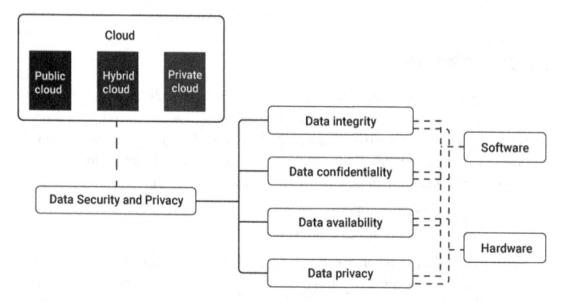

Figure 5-14. *Identity and Access Management (IAM) in Azure*

- Password management

- Multifactor Authentication(MFA): Multifactor authentication is an electronic authentication method in which a user can access the application or data only after providing two or more pieces of information—what the user knows, such as a password, what the user has, such as a token, and what the user is, using biometric verification.

- Role-based access control (RBAC): Role-based access control is a method for controlling what users can do within a company's IT application. RBAC enables access control by assigning roles to end users. See Figure 5-15.

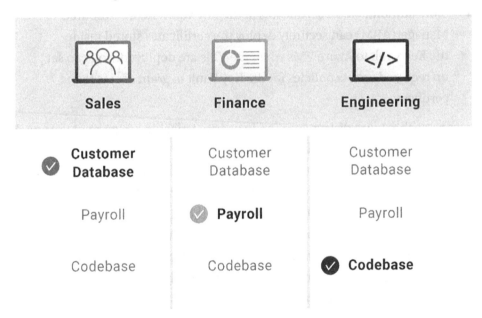

Figure 5-15. *Role-based access control*

- Conditional access policies

- Monitor suspicious activities

Another important consideration for protecting data is to select the right key management solution. Azure Key Vault (AKV) safeguards keys, certificates, and secrets that can be used by cloud applications and services. Azure Key Vault is designed to store keys and secrets. It is not intended to store the passwords.

Best practices for using Azure Key Vault to store data are as follows:

- Grant access to the users, groups, or application for specific purposes.

- Azure has many in-built roles as well and you can create custom roles as per the requirements. You can assign those predefined roles to users or groups as needed.

- Control users who have access to the data or application.

- Access to Key Vault is managed through two separate interfaces: management plane and data plane. For example, if you want to grant data plane access permissions using the Key Vault access policies then no management plane access is needed for the application.

- Store authentication certificates in the Key Vault: Azure Resource Manager(ARM) can securely deploy the certificates stored inside the Key Vault to Azure VMs when the VMs are deployed. You can set up required access policies for the Key Vault to grant access to the certificate.

You can use the Azure disk encryption in a virtual machine to encrypt the attached disks on the Windows or Linux VMs. Azure Storage uses Azure storage encryption to encrypt data at rest in the Azure Storage. Encryption, decryption, and key management are transparent to end users. Azure SQL databases and Azure Synapse Analytics use Transparent Data Encryption (TDE) to execute the real-time encryption and decryption of the database, related backup, and transaction log files without requiring any changes to the application. SQL databases also have a feature called Always Encrypted to protect sensitive data at rest and on the server. This prevents Database Administrators (DBAs), cloud database operators, and other high privileged non-authorized users from accessing encrypted data directly from the server as well.

Network Security for Data Access

In order to protect data in transit, you can use Secure Socket Layer (SSL)/Transport Layer Security (TLS) certificates while exchanging data across locations. You can isolate the communication channel between the on-premises and cloud infrastructure using the Virtual Private Network (VPN) or Express Route (ER).

Using the network security groups (NSGs), you can reduce the number of potential attacks, as the network security groups contain a list of security rules that allow or deny inbound or outbound network traffic based on destination address, source ports, destination ports, or protocol. VMs within the two Azure virtual networks can easily talk to each other using VNET peering. Network traffic between the peered virtual networks is private.

Monitoring

Microsoft Defender for Cloud automatically collects, analyzes, and integrates logs from the Azure resources, networks, and solutions such as firewalls. See Figure 5-16.

Figure 5-16. *Microsoft Defender for Cloud*

Log analytics provide centralized access to the logs and help analyze the log data to create custom alerts for proactive monitoring. It is the primary tool for editing the log queries and interactively analyzing the results. From the portal, you can use and interactively execute queries and sort, filter, and analyze the logs. See Figure 5-17.

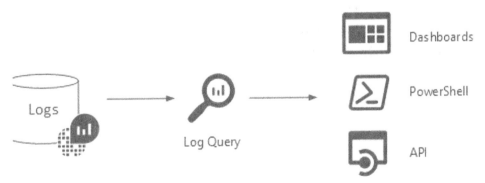

Figure 5-17. *Log analytics workspace*

Azure SQL Database and threat protection detects abnormal activities and identifies attempts to get unauthorized access to the data, database, or system. Security officers and administrators get immediate notifications about abnormal activities so they can take required actions in a timely manner. See Figure 5-18.

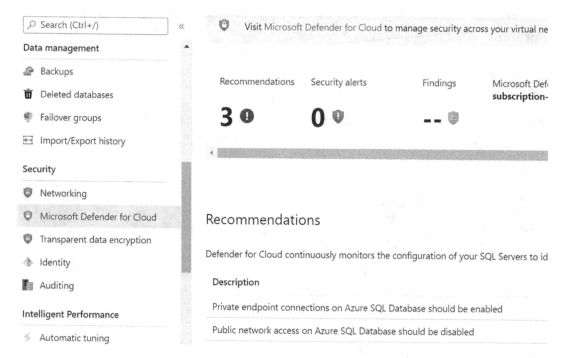

Figure 5-18. *Microsoft Defender for Cloud*

Advanced Threat Protection (ATP) for Azure SQL Database can identify potential SQL injections, access attempts from unusual location or data centers, and brute force attacks on the SQL database. Once Advanced Threat Protection is configured, it will automatically detect these threats via email notifications or via the Azure Portal. Advanced Threat Protection is part of Microsoft Defender for SQL. It can be accessed from the SQL Server Portal or from the central Microsoft Defender portal. See Figure 5-19.

○ Refresh   ↓ Download CSV report   ⌁ Open query   ☑ Governance report (preview)   ⼈ Guides & Feedback

Secure score recommendations   **All recommendations**

Active recommendations (by severity)

High	Medium	Low
6/23	17/30	3/17

Resource health

▮ Unhealthy (45)   ▮ Healthy (10)   ▮ Not applicable (18)

⌕ Search recommendations

Recommendation status == **None** ✕   Severity == **None** ✕

Recommendation maturity == **None** ✕   Owner == **None** ✕

Figure 5-19. *Advanced Threat Protection*

Data Encryption Patterns

When data is in the cloud, it resides inside the cloud storage, in memory, or on the network during the transit. With a cloud solution, a single transaction can lead to multiple data operations whereby the data moves from one storage medium to another. In order to provide full data protection and security, the data must be encrypted on the storage volumes. See Figure 5-20.

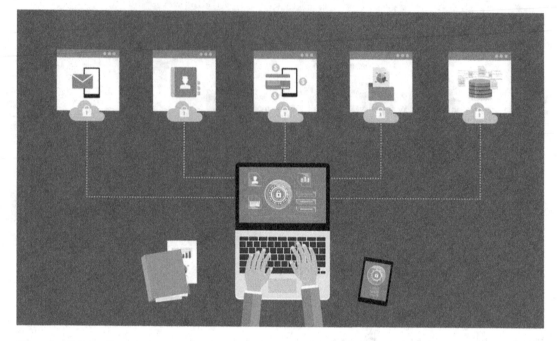

Figure 5-20. *Data encryption*

A few major points to consider with data encryption:

- Use identity-based storage access controls

- Encrypt the virtual disks for the virtual machines

- Use secure hash algorithms for data encryption

- Protect data in transit by using encrypted network channels like HTTPS or TLS for client-server communication

- Use additional key encryption key (KEK) to protect the data encryption key (DEK)

Microsoft Azure has built-in data encryption features in many layers and also participates in data processing. Microsoft recommends you enable the encryption capability for all Microsoft services to protect and secure your data.

Cloud storage is very well architected and implemented differently than traditional on-premises solutions. It enables massive scaling and modern access via the REST API and isolation between the tenants. All Azure storage services have various built-in data encryption features to protect and secure data (see Table 5-1).

- Identity based access control: You can enable access to the storage service using the Azure Active Directory and key-based authentications, such as storage account access key and shared access signature (SAS).

- Built-in storage encryption: All cloud storage data is by default encrypted. Data can't be read by the tenant if it hasn't been written by the tenant. With this feature, you can make sure that data isn't leaked.

- Region-based controls: Data only remains in the selected region and three copies of the data is maintained in other regions. Azure storage has detailed activity logging available based on the configuration.

- Firewall features: Azure Firewall provides an additional layer of access control and storage threat protection to detect abnormal activities related to access.

Table 5-1. *Azure's Key Management Parameters*

Key management parameter	Microsoft-managed keys	Customer-managed keys	Customer-provided keys
Encryption/decryption operations	Azure	Azure	Azure
Azure Storage services supported	All	Blob storage, Azure Files[1,2]	Blob storage
Key storage	Microsoft key store	Azure Key Vault or Key Vault HSM	Customer's own key store
Key rotation responsibility	Microsoft	Customer	Customer
Key control	Microsoft	Customer	Customer

In order to better understand how Microsoft Azure implements encryption at rest, you need to understand the various encryption models. These definitions are shared across all resource providers to ensure a common language:

- Server-side encryption using service-managed keys: In this method of encryption, encryption is mainly performed by the Azure service, which is basically done by the Microsoft Azure cloud resource provider. Consider an example where Azure Storage receives the data in plain text format and encryption and decryption are performed automatically by the cloud service providers when you write or read data to the Azure storage account. Resource providers can use their own encryption key or they can use a custom encryption key, depending on the storage encryption configuration. See Figure 5-21.

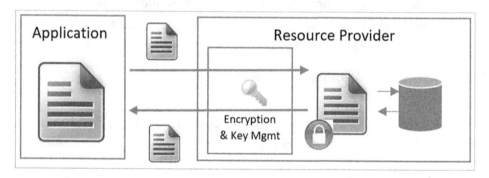

Figure 5-21. *Server-side encryption*

- Client encryption model: This encryption model is performed outside Azure by the service or client application. With this setup, Azure resource providers can encrypt the blob of data, but they can't decrypt the data or access the encryption keys. See Figure 5-22.

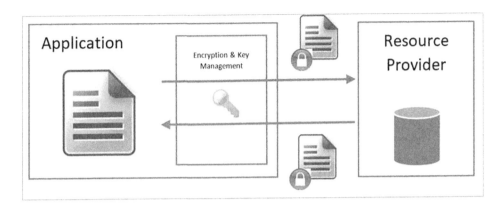

Figure 5-22. *Client-side encryption*

Some Azure services store the root key encryption key (KEK) in the Azure Key Vault and store the encrypted data encryption key (DEK) in the internal location where the data resides.

Conclusion

This chapter discussed securing the data stored in the cloud. You also learned about the various ways to classify the data and make it available for downstream users and applications in a secure manner. You also learned about the various data encryption patterns and related models when working with public cloud providers like Azure, Google, AWS, and so on.

CHAPTER 6

Security Processes

Every modern enterprise uses a large amount and variety of data to work on various data-driven initiatives. Having various security processes in place is a must in order to properly and safely use data and create business insights from it.

The previous chapter discussed various patterns for building applications on the cloud. You also took a quick tour of various data security patterns that provide easier and safer access to the data stored in the cloud.

This chapter covers the following topics:

- Complete mediation with threat modeling

- Securing the infrastructure and application deployment

- Security testing

- Key management

- Vulnerability management

- Disaster recovery

Complete Meditation with Threat Modeling

Every company has a dedicated infrastructure and networking team. The application development team focuses more on the development lifecycle and leaves the security assessments and controls to the infrastructure and networking team. The majority of the developers think this way due to the following reasons:

- Security is implemented from Layer 2/Layer 3/Layer 4 of OSI model, as shown in Figure 6-1, and there are various security layers: Physical Security, Perimeter and Network Security, Secure Endpoints, Application Security, Data Security, and Mission-Critical Assets.

© Sagar Lad 2023
S. Lad, *Azure Security For Critical Workloads*, https://doi.org/10.1007/978-1-4842-8936-5_6

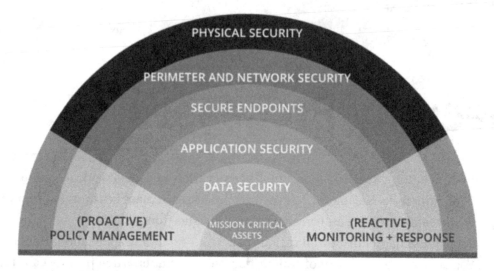

Figure 6-1. *Security layers*

- Fault isolation and resiliency weren't considered during the design phase.

As displayed in Figure 6-2, thread modeling is an iterative process that starts by defining the threat, creating the threat modeling diagram, identifying the relevant threats, mitigating the threats, and validate them to see if the relevant threat is resolved.

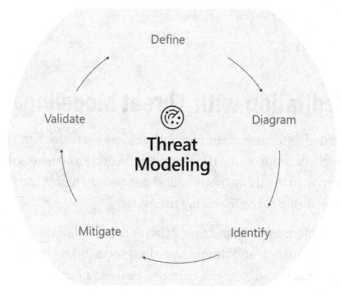

Figure 6-2. *Threat modeling process*

Things are changing fast due to greater public cloud adoption. In the past few years, distributed architecture coupled with DevOps has put forth new requirements like resiliency and fault isolation on applications and services. Application and services need to continue functioning correctly even in the presence of faults in underlying layers. This is also due to the fact that hardware and networks are moving to a commodity model leveraging PaaS models with on premises and public cloud options. Nonfunctional requirements (NFRs) like fault isolation and resiliency are becoming the norm of every application and service. This changing need has also put more focus on "security by design," bringing in the need to implement the security controls from within the application and services.

Enterprises need to determine the security controls which need to be implemented in the application and services. Security controls are not an IT need but a business need and hence the security controls need to be done in the frame of "business risk assessment", modeling threats with a focus on business impact. A beautiful approach to modeling security threats for your application and services is the STRIDE model. With this model, we can answer the questions like "What are the security threats in my application and services and what security controls does my team need to implement for an application or service?".

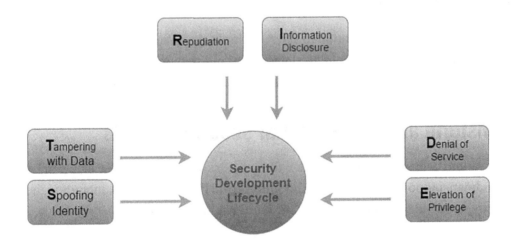

STRIDE Threat Model

Figure 6-3. *STRIDE threat modeling*

Threat modeling is a process of creating an optimized application by identifying the objectives and security vulnerabilities to prevent the security issues to the application. It helps to identify the security requirements of the system or application which is mission critical and contains sensitive data. It provides a systematic and structured process to identify potential threats and the security vulnerabilities to reduce the risk of the IT resources.

With respect to software security, threat modeling is considered to be a very critical activity of the software design and development. Without evaluating and migrating the threats, it is impossible to build applications and systems which comply with the corporate security policies and regulatory requirements.

We look at the process of threat modeling in the next sections.

Form a Team

The team should include stakeholders, business developers, owners, and security experts. People from diverse backgrounds make the threat modeling process more robust and secure.

Define the Scope

Define the scope of the application to start the threat-modeling process. For example, does the developed application focus on applications, networks, or infrastructures? You can create a catalogue of all components and map them to the architecture diagrams.

Brainstorm and List Potential Security Threats

For all system components, determine if threats exist. With this exercise, you can build the roadmap, pinpoint the expected and unexpected threat scenarios, including the threat trees, and identify possible weakness and vulnerabilities.

Prioritize Threats

Determine the level of the threats and rank them to take appropriate risk-mitigation actions. One common approach to determining priority is to multiply the damage potential of the threat by its likelihood of happening.

Develop and Implement Risk Mitigation

Decide how to mitigate each threat or reduce the risk to an acceptable level to avoid any issues with the security measures. You can transfer the risk, reduce the risk, or accept the risk.

Document the Results

You can document all the findings of the threat-modeling process and related actions so future changes to the application, landscape, and the operating environment can assess and update the threat model. See Figure 6-4.

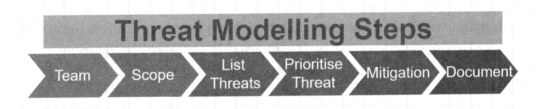

Figure 6-4. *Threat-modeling steps*

The threat modeling (aka the STRIDE) model works on the principle of data flows and trust boundaries. Each security threat in the STRIDE model is a potential violation that needs to be accessed for vulnerabilities in your application and system. If the risks are viable, you must implement the security controls.

Each letter of STRIDE stands for a security threat and is linked to a desired property. Here are the details:

S = Spoofing (linked to the authenticity of your application and services)

T = Tampering (linked to the integrity of the data)

R = Repudiation (linked to the beautiful requirement of non-repudiation)

I = Information disclosure (linked to the confidentiality of your data or parts of application and services)

D = Denial of service (linked to the availability of your application and services)

E = Elevation of privilege (linked to the authorization of your application and services)

STRIDE modeling must be done at the design phase and revisited in the development and testing phases. Security needs to be done from the perspective of capturing all requirements as early as possible. The STRIDE model discusses the potential security risk per threat and marks them against their probability and impact. The risks are seen from inside as well as outside attack vectors. The STRIDE model can reveal threats and, with proper analysis, the trust boundaries can be determined and security controls that need to be implemented can be captured.

It is best to couple STRIDE threat modeling with pattern-based security. Based on the trust boundaries identified from the threat modeling, you can map the security controls to a particular security zone and then implement the controls aligned to this security zone. This keeps security zones and security controls centralized and brings the security team closer to engineers. In addition to this, the model is easily to for any new application or service. The beauty of this approach from an architectural perspective is simplicity while serving the requirements of fault isolation and resiliency for the applications and services across the Development, Test, Acceptance, and Production (DTAP) environments.

After looking at the threat modeling process and its steps in detail, it's now time to dive into how you can secure the infrastructure and application deployment process.

Securing the Infrastructure and Application Deployment

Every enterprise must have a well-defined software development lifecycle process to deploy applications securely with proper security checks in place during the design, development, testing, and deployment stages. It is best to create a layered system architecture that uses standard frameworks to design an application for the identity, authorization, and access control. Let's look at a few options to improve security of the infrastructure and application deployment.

Automate Security Releases

Considering the wide range of security vulnerabilities, it is very difficult to deploy, update, and patch application environments to meet security standards without using the automated security tools. In order to automate the security releases, it is best to create continuous integration/continuous deployment pipelines (CI/CD). One advantage of creating automated CI/CD pipelines is that you remove the manual errors, provide a standardized development feedback loop, and increase the speed of deployment for the new features. You can also use automation to scan the security vulnerabilities when the artefacts are created and define policies for different environments (development, test, acceptance and production—DTAP) to verify that the artefacts have been deployed. See Figure 6-5.

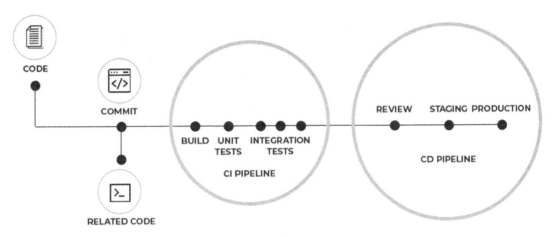

Figure 6-5. *Automated security with CI/CD pipeline*

There are certain considerations while automating security with CI/CD pipelines. You need to protect the CI/CD pipeline using Access Control.

You need to start by defining who can send code changes to the repository, which will be used as a storage base to ensure the first layer of protection for the automated pipeline. You also need to ensure what is sent, stored, and moved into the CI/CD pipeline. Another point to ensure is that the security of the process occurs with the least possible intervention. See Figure 6-6.

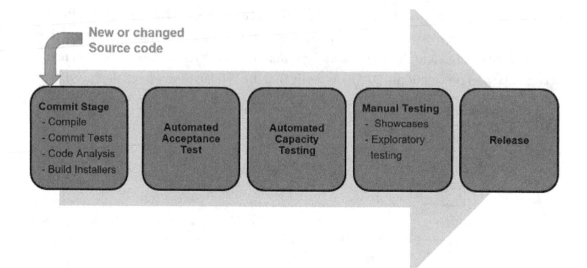

Figure 6-6. *Automated CI/CD pipeline configuration*

Well-Governed Application Deployment

If an attacker compromises the CI/CD pipeline, the entire technology stack can have a major impact. In order to secure the pipeline, you need to enforce the established approval process to deploy the code into production. See Figure 6-7.

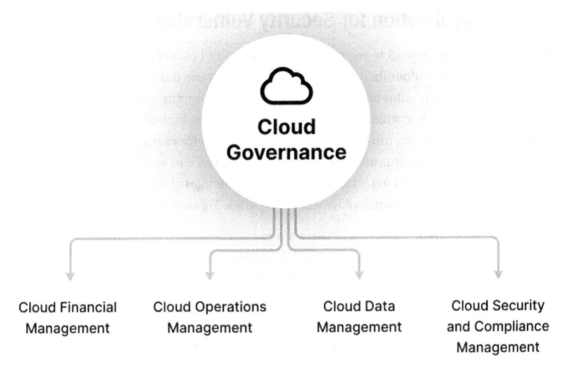

Figure 6-7. *Application deployment governance*

Scan Security Vulnerabilities

It is best to use automated tools to continuously perform a vulnerability scan before packages/containers are deployed to the production environment. See Figure 6-8.

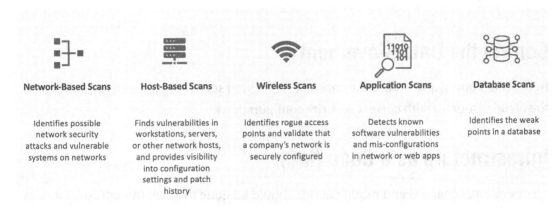

Figure 6-8. *Security vulnerability scans*

Monitor Application for Security Vulnerabilities

In order to proactively react to security vulnerabilities, it's best to constantly monitor the application code for vulnerabilities. For example, you can use the web security scanner to identify the security vulnerabilities in the app engine, compute engine, or web applications. This web scanner helps identify vulnerabilities, including XSS (cross-site scripting), Flash injection, mixed content (HTTP in HTTPS for example), and insecure libraries. If you have a monitoring mechanism in place, you can easily detect such vulnerabilities beforehand to tackle those security challenges at the early stage of the application development and deployment process. See Figure 6-9.

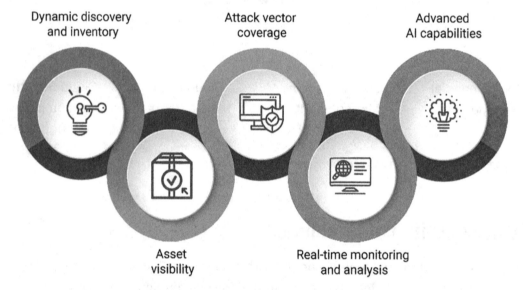

Figure 6-9. *Security vulnerability management*

Control the Data Movement

In order to control and secure the data stored in cloud services, you need to configure the cloud resources with correct security configurations.

Infrastructure as a Code (IaC)

All operational changes and modifications should be done through the Infrastructure as a Code pipelines. IaC is a key DevOps practice and it is often used to enable continuous integration and delivery. See Figure 6-10.

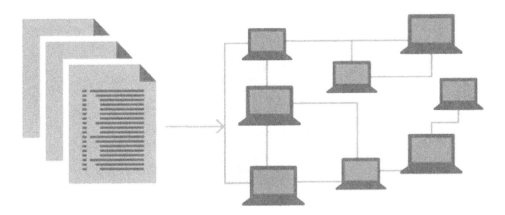

Figure 6-10. *Infrastructure as a Code*

It reduces the manual effort required to do all the configurations and automate the environment deployment using the Infrastructure as a code pipeline. It is a vital practice for the DevOps adoption. It makes the release changes to the production faster and reduces the time to market.

Pipeline Secret Management

Confidential certificates, keys, and secrets used in the deployment pipeline should be stored in the Key Vault (AKV). When you do the deployment of the application infrastructure with the Azure Resource Manager (ARM), Bicep or Terraform, you have various credentials to connect to different services. It is best to use confidential secrets from the secret management tools like Key Vault (AKV) instead of hard coding these values. See Figure 6-11.

Figure 6-11. *Azure Key Vault for Pipeline secrets*

Adhere to the Principle of Least Privilege

Based on the principle of least privilege, the main goal is to grant only required permissions. If possible, it is also best to grant access to the roles and not to the individual users. Restrict the access as much as possible:

1. Restrict admin access to users as much as possible

2. Users with higher access can change security objects such as roles, users, or permission management

3. Roles that have capability to add, change, or remove security privileges

The principle of least privileged access means that users are only given the privileges that they need to perform their jobs efficiently.

Let's now look at how to perform security testing on an application.

Security Testing

With cloud computing, you can access and use IT resources over the Internet with the pay-as-you-use cost principle. You can access technology and cloud services using the compute power, storage, and databases instead of buying, owning, and maintaining physical data centers and servers. There are many public cloud providers available in the market, including Azure, Google Cloud, and AWS. See Figure 6-12.

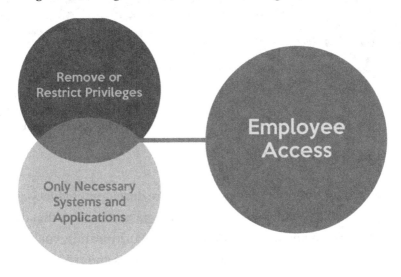

Figure 6-12. *Public cloud providers*

As cloud provider popularity increases day by day, attackers focus more on cloud services and security vulnerabilities. Attackers use security attacks against these managed cloud service providers. Enterprise organizations should focus on securing cloud resources.

In order to avoid cloud security attacks, it is best to enable cloud penetration testing, which is an attack performed to find security vulnerabilities that could cause issues or misconfigurations in a cloud-based system. See Figure 6-13.

Figure 6-13. *Cloud security testing*

Security testing is an essential step in the software development lifecycle. In security testing, it uncovers security vulnerabilities of the system and ensures that data and system resources are protected from attackers. With security testing, you can also ensure that software systems and applications are free from threats and risks.

The main goal of security testing is as follows:

- Identify the threats in the system

- Measure and detect security vulnerabilities on time

- Proactively detect every possible security risk in the system

- Enable integration with third-party tools for code scanning and vulnerabilities

During security testing, the main goal of the principles are as follows (see Figure 6-14):

- Confidentiality

- Integrity

- Authentication

- Authorization

- Availability

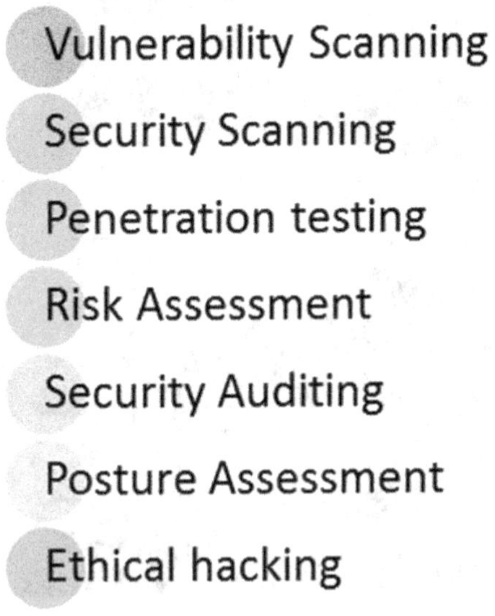

Vulnerability Scanning

Security Scanning

Penetration testing

Risk Assessment

Security Auditing

Posture Assessment

Ethical hacking

Figure 6-14. Security testing types

Let's look at the types of security testing.

Vulnerability Testing

It is best to enable this type of testing performed with the help of an automated software. The main goal is to scan the entire system and application to detect the known vulnerabilities.

Security Scanning

During security scanning, the main goal is to identify network and system weaknesses. This type of scanning provides solutions for reducing the risks or defects.

Penetration Testing

With penetration testing, the main goal is to simulate attacks from attackers to tackle those challenges proactively. This includes an analysis of the system to examine potential vulnerabilities from the hacker to hack the system. See Figure 6-15.

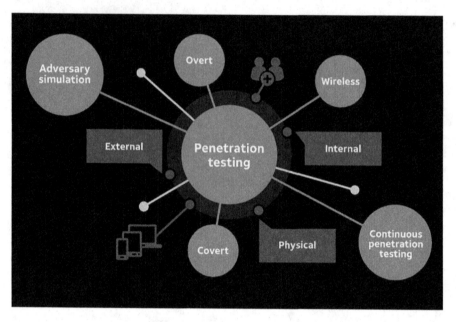

Figure 6-15. *Penetration testing*

Risk Assessment

Risk assessment mainly consists of security risks that were observed in the organization to determine the likelihood and the impact of the risk. Risks are divided into the three types: low, medium, and high. See Figure 6-16.

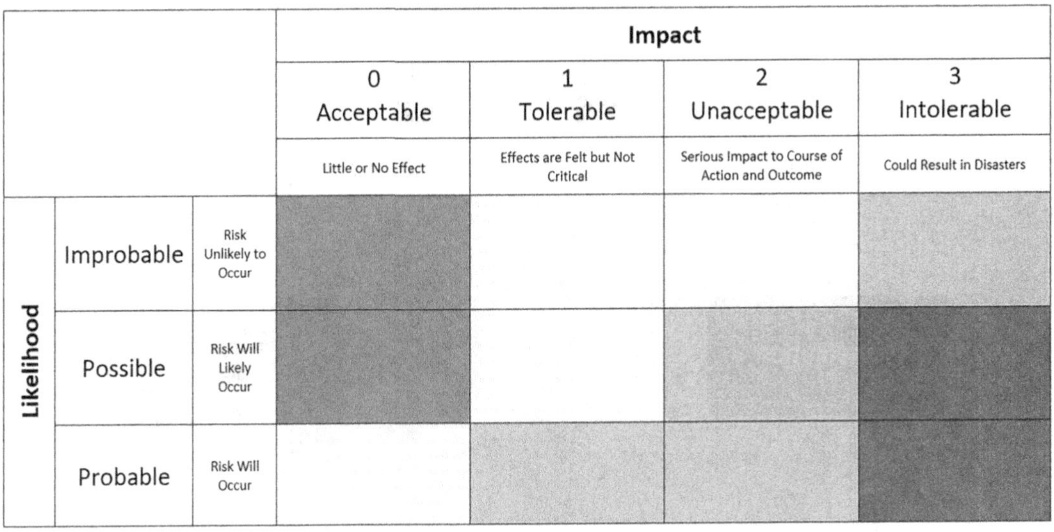

			Impact			
			0 Acceptable	1 Tolerable	2 Unacceptable	3 Intolerable
			Little or No Effect	Effects are Felt but Not Critical	Serious Impact to Course of Action and Outcome	Could Result in Disasters
Likelihood	Improbable	Risk Unlikely to Occur				
	Possible	Risk Will Likely Occur				
	Probable	Risk Will Occur				

Figure 6-16. *Risk assessment matrix*

Security Auditing

Security auditing is an internal inspection of the software application and OS to identify security defects. Security audits can be performed in various ways by looking at the code line by line. You can start by the planning, scoping, and logistics of the security auditing to be placed across the applications. The next step is to collect data and gather evidence. Once the data is collected, you perform the analysis, interpret the data, and generate the reports. Once that is done, you create an action plan to fix those findings. See Figure 6-17.

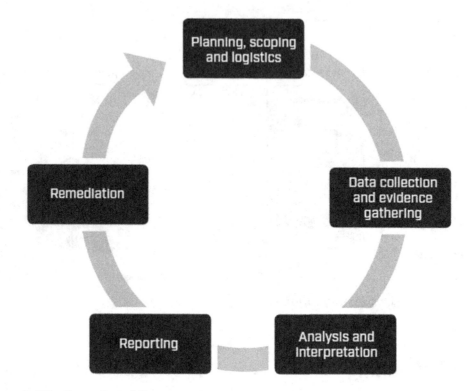

Figure 6-17. *Security audit process*

Ethical Hacking

The purpose of ethical hacking is to expose security flaws in the system. It involves an authorized attempt to get unauthorized access to an application, system, or data.

Ethical hacking follows these four concepts:

- Legal: Gather approval to access and perform the security assessment.

- Define scope: Determine the scope to perform the ethical hacking so that hacking activities will remain legal and within the organization's approved boundaries.

- Record vulnerabilities: Once all the vulnerabilities are recorded, notify the organization of all the vulnerabilities and take action to prevent the security issues.

- Posture assessment: This is a combination of ethical hacking, security scanning, and risk assessments to provide an overall security of the organization. This assessment is done to ensure that cybersecurity practices are followed in the organization. Data breaches, cyberattacks, and online threats have become major threats for many organizations. Security posture assessment is calculated based on resources such as people, hardware, and software capabilities whenever a new virus attacks. It shows the security health of the product or the application. There are various levels of the assessment, which indirectly mean posture assessment. See Figure 6-18.

Figure 6-18. *Posture assessment*

After understanding the types of security testing, let's look at the process of security testing. You must include a security testing phase in the software development lifecycle phase. See Figure 6-19.

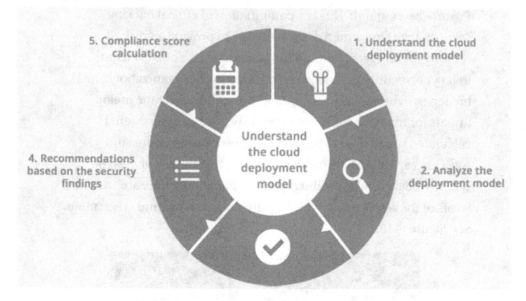

Figure 6-19. *Security testing process*

Requirements

Gather requirements for the security analysis to check if the application is compatible with the security standards.

Design

Security test plans should be designed and include the development plan for all security tests.

Unit Testing

This is the smallest, testable part of an application that can be individually tested to ensure functionality. See Figure 6-20.

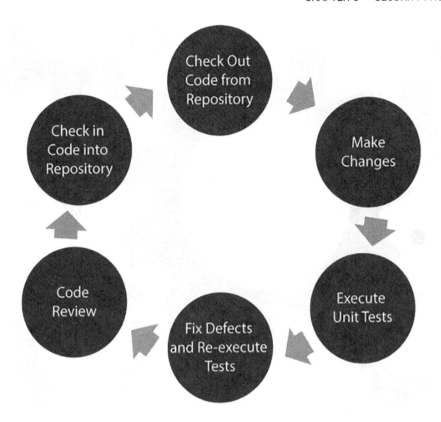

Figure 6-20. *Unit testing*

Integration Testing

Integration testing is a type of software testing in which different units, modules, or components of the software applications are tested as a combined entity. See Figure 6-21.

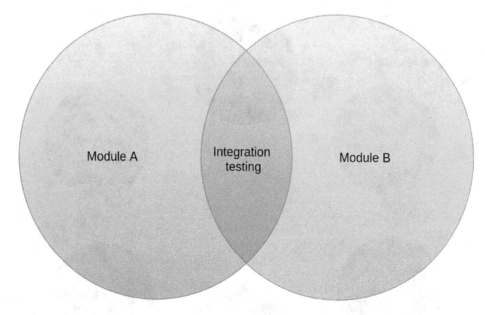

Figure 6-21. *Integration testing*

System Testing

System testing, also referred to as system-level testing, is where the quality assurance team evaluates how various components of an application interact together in the full, integrated system or application. System testing verifies that an application performs its tasks as designed. It mainly focuses on the functionality of the application.

System testing examines every component of the application to ensure that it works as an application as a whole. The QA team typically conducts the system testing after the individual modules with functional or user-story testing is performed.

There are various tools available in the market by which you can perform the system testing. These tools can create, manage, and automate test cases and it also has additional features other than testing.

- Implementation: In the implementation phase, you perform thorough penetration testing and vulnerability scanning to execute and detect any vulnerabilities.

- Support: Once the vulnerabilities are identified and detected, the next step is to mitigate them to make sure the system is free from vulnerabilities. See Figure 6-22.

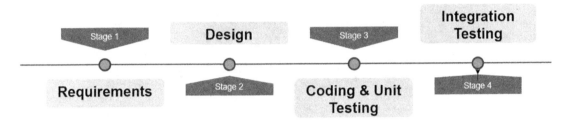

Figure 6-22. *System testing phases*

Now that you understand the security testing process, let's take a quick tour of the key management process.

Key Management

Confidential secrets and keys are an important part of any security system. Using keys, you can perform encryption and decryption of the user authentication. See Figure 6-23.

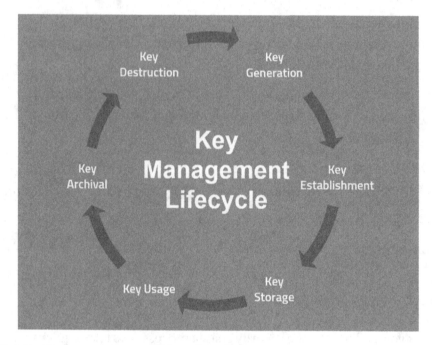

Figure 6-23. *Key management lifecycle*

Proper management of the keys and their related components can ensure the safety of confidential information. Key management is the process of putting standards in place to ensure the security of confidential information. With key management, you can create, exchange, store, delete, and refresh the keys.

Key management is one of the foundational building blocks of all data security. Data is encrypted and decrypted using encryption keys. If the keys are lost, there will be an impact on accessing the data. Keys also ensure the safe transmission of the data across an Internet connection. See Figure 6-24.

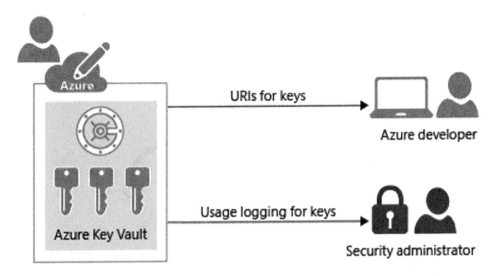

Figure 6-24. *Azure Key Vault: Secret management*

There are two types of keys: symmetric and asymmetric. Symmetric keys deal with the data at rest, which is stored in a static location such as a database. Symmetric encryption uses the same key for encryption and decryption. Encryption using an asymmetric key is more complicated than symmetric encryption. Instead of using the same key, it uses a public key and private key to encrypt and decrypt the data. This public key can be shared with anyone since it encrypts the data but you can't decrypt the data. See Figure 6-25.

Symmetric Encryption

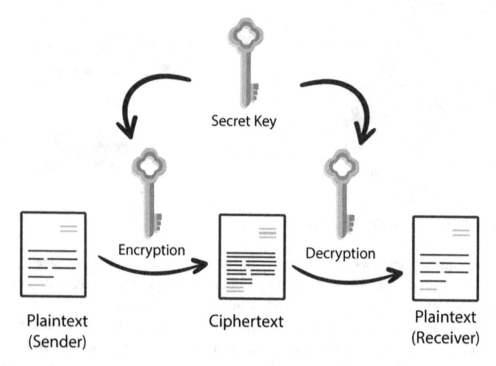

Figure 6-25. *Symmetric encryption*

Asymmetric encryption focuses on encrypting data in motion. Data in motion means the data that is sent across a network connection, which can be a private or public connection. For most data-transmission activities, asymmetric keys are used to protect sensitive data.

Key management follows a lifecycle process for which you need to ensure that the keys are created, stored, used, and rotated securely. Most cryptographic keys follow a lifecycle that involves the following:

- Generation

- Distribution

- Use

- Storage

- Rotation

- Backup

- Destruction

Irrespective of the key management process that organizations follow, a major challenge is to make sure keys are stored securely and are not being misused by unauthorized people. The following are recommended practices to ensure compliance with government regulation and standards.

- Avoid hard-coded keys: It's best not to hard-code values into the source code. Anyone with access to the code can access that confidential information.

- Hardware Security Module (HSM): HSMs are dedicated processors typically designed for the protection of the crypto key lifecycle. They act as a security module that creates trust anchors that protect the cryptographic infrastructure of the organization. HSM is a secure, cryptographic processor designed specifically to protect the lifecycle of the confidential keys. It provides a high level of security in terms of confidentiality, integrity, and availability. See Figure 6-26.

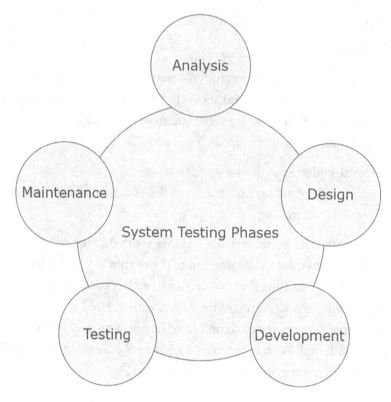

Figure 6-26. *Hardware Security Module (HSM)*

Next, we explore vulnerability management and discuss how you can efficiently detect and handle it.

Vulnerability Management

Patching your application and system with daily, weekly, and monthly updates is a humongous task. Moreover, in the period between patches, depending on the severity of the pending vulnerability, a bug can become a weakness in the application or system.

Keeping virtual machines and devices up-to-date is mandatory to create secure software applications. If the virtual machines or devices are outdated, that leaves the software applications exposed to cyberattacks. Thus, it is very important that vulnerabilities be patched as soon as possible. It is also important to manage patches and vulnerability detection so that severe problems are detected quickly.

A majority of the malware issues are sent via emails. This malicious software can come in multiple forms: worms, viruses, trojans, and ransomware. Worms are a type of malware that spreads from computer to network without user intervention. Computer viruses are malware that affects digital media such as computer memory.

A trojan horse is downloaded on to a system when the user downloads a program or opens an email containing a malicious attachment. Attackers usually use these to steal privileged information, like passwords, from the system. Ransomware is a kind of malicious software that is created to block access to files or directories on an infected computer, after which the attacker demands that the victim pay money to get their files back.

Vulnerability management is a process of identifying, evaluating, and reporting security vulnerabilities in the system and software that runs on them. It refers to the weakness that allows an attacker to get access to the product and the information it holds. It is an ongoing process of identifying, assessing, reporting, and managing security vulnerabilities across workloads, systems, and endpoints.

Security vulnerabilities refer to technological weakness that allow attackers to compromise a product or application. The vulnerability management process can be broken into these four steps:

- Identifying vulnerabilities

- Evaluating vulnerabilities

- Treating vulnerabilities

- Reporting vulnerabilities

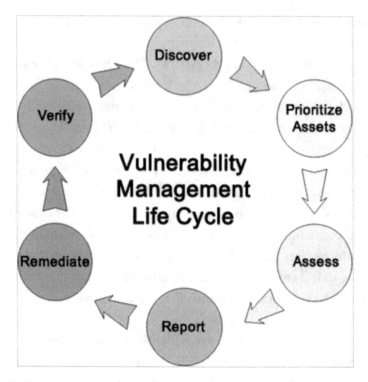

Figure 6-27. *Vulnerability management*

The steps of the vulnerability lifecycle are as follows:

- Discover: The first step is to identify the inventory of all assets across the network and identify host details, including the operating system and open services to identify vulnerabilities. Develop a network baseline and identify security vulnerabilities on a regular automated schedule.

- Prioritize assets: Categorize assets into group or business units and assign the business value to asset groups based on the priority and criticality of the business operation.

- Assess: Determine the baseline risk profile so you can eliminate risk based on criticality, vulnerability, and asset classification. This will help reduce the vulnerability of the developed application.

- Report: Once the vulnerabilities are assessed, measure the risk based on the security policies. Create a security plan, monitor the activities, and describe the known vulnerabilities.

- Remediate: Once the report is ready, prioritize and fix the vulnerabilities according to the business risk. Once that is done, establish the control and show the progress.

- Verification: The last step is to verify that the threats have been eliminated through the audits. See Figure 6-28.

Key phases of a secret's lifecycle

| Creation | Storage | Rotation | Revocation |

Figure 6-28. *Vulnerability report*

Vulnerability can be defined as a weakness of an asset or group of assets that can be exploited by one or more threats. Any means or act by which an external actor gets unauthorized access to the data or privilege to control an application is considered a vulnerability. Common examples include communication network ports that are open to the Internet and insecure configurations of software and OSs. At a higher level, vulnerabilities can be broken into a few components:

- CVE - Common Vulnerabilities and Exposure: Each CVE defines a specific vulnerability that attackers can attack on the application or system.

- CCE - Common Configuration Enumeration: This is a list of system security configuration issues that can be used to develop configuration guidance.

- CPE - Common Platform Enumeration: This is a standardized method of describing and identifying classes of the application, operating systems, and devices in the environment.

- CVSS - Common Vulnerability Scoring System: This scoring system assigns the scores to each defined vulnerability and is used to prioritize efforts and resources according to the threat.

Disaster Recovery (DR)

Disaster recovery is the process of restoring application functionality during an abnormal situation. Upfront failures can happen at any point in time when you use public clouds like Azure, AWS, or GCP. When such failures occur, you should be able to minimize the effect of failing components. See Figure 6-29.

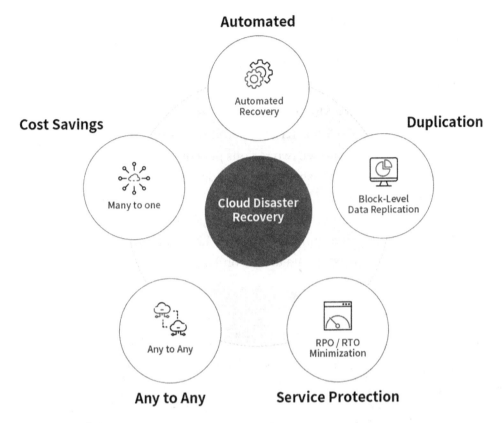

Figure 6-29. Disaster recovery management

With automated testing, you can prepare and minimize failures. A standard backup and recovery process is a must in order to handle such failures without an impact. You need to consider the following key points while creating a disaster and recovery plan:

- Create a disaster and recovery plan considering all failure scenarios

- Design a disaster recovery plan to run most applications with reduced functionality

- Design a backup strategy tailored to your business requirements

- Automate processes and runbooks to do the rollback or failover activities

After understanding the basics of backup and disaster recovery, let's look at the disaster recovery process of design and implementation.

- Determine subscription and service requirements: The process of determining the subscription and service requirements consists of various key processes. Certain resources, such as resource groups and storage accounts, are limited in every Azure subscription.

- Azure regional pairs: Multiple regional pairs are accessible in Azure. For example, North China, East China, North Europe, and West Europe, where you can see two regions per continent. Some Azure services can take advantage of cross-region replication to ensure business continuity and protect against data loss. Azure provides several storage solutions that use cross-region replication to ensure data availability. For example, Azure Geo Redundant storage automatically replicates data to a secondary region. See Figure 6-30.

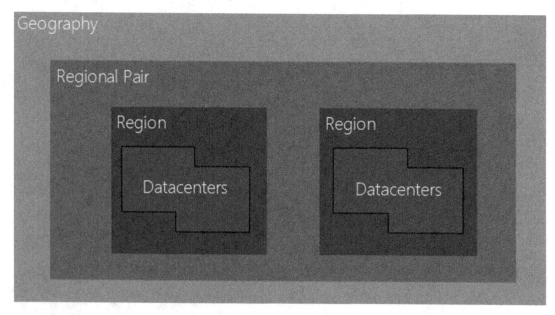

Figure 6-30. *Azure regional pairs*

- Azure availability zones: Availability zones are dedicated physical locations in an Azure region. In order to ensure resiliency, three separate zones are enabled in every region. See Figure 6-31.

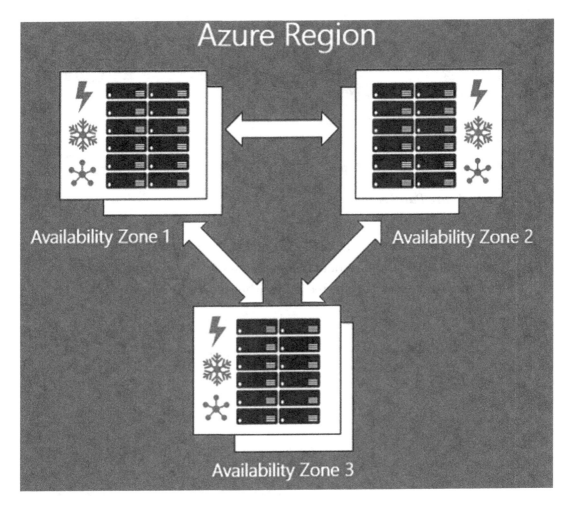

Figure 6-31. *Azure availability zones*

- Azure PaaS components: Azure provides many built-in PaaS services. Each service can be configured to enable backup and georeplication in case there are issues. See Figure 6-32.

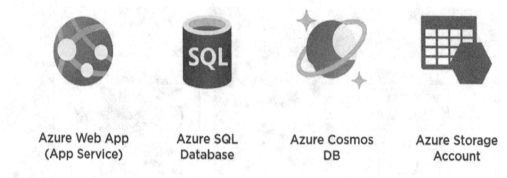

Azure Web App   **Azure SQL**   **Azure Cosmos**   **Azure Storage**
  (App Service)   **Database**   **DB**   **Account**

Figure 6-32. *Azure PaaS services*

- Determine and document RTO, RPO, and RLO: Recovery Time objective (RTO) is the amount of time and service level within which business processes must be recovered when a disaster happens. See Figure 6-33.

Figure 6-33. *Recovery Time Objective*

Recovery Point Objective (RPO) refers to the amount of time that can be lost before creating damage to the organization. Recovery Level Objective (RLO) specifies the granularity by which data must be recovered.

Conclusion

This chapter explored the threat modeling process and the need to enable it in your organization. You also learned about how to secure your infrastructure and platform deployment with the Infrastructure as a Code (IaC). Then you learned the importance of the security testing process and its related phases. Then you learned about the importance of the key management process and standard process to automate it.

The chapter also discussed vulnerability management and the importance of the disaster recovery process and its best practices.

CHAPTER 7

Automated Security Monitoring

Security monitoring is the automated process of collecting and analyzing potential security threats and taking appropriate actions to create secure applications. Nowadays, more and more companies are entering the market with cloud adoptions. Monitoring this cloud workload is a must in order to create secure and safe applications.

The previous chapter took a quick tour of threat modelling and securing infrastructure deployment, including security testing, key management, and disaster recovery.

This chapter covers the following topics:

- Setting up security policies

- Advanced observability

- Azure Monitor

- Azure Sentinel

Setting Up Security Policies

Microsoft Defender applies security initiatives to Azure subscriptions. These initiatives contain security policies that can be enforced at a subscription level or resource group level. Every security policy includes things like the type of resources that can be deployed and enforces the tags for all resources. As shown in Figure 7-1, you can view policy definitions and initiatives on the Azure Portal.

© Sagar Lad 2023
S. Lad, *Azure Security For Critical Workloads*, https://doi.org/10.1007/978-1-4842-8936-5_7

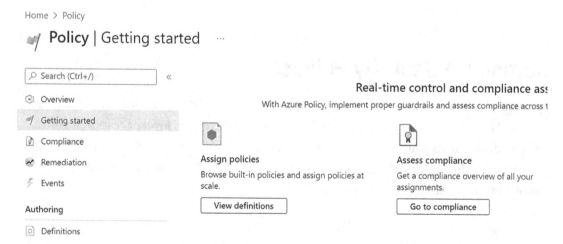

Figure 7-1. *Security policies and initiatives*

   – Security policy: An Azure security policy is a rule about the specific
     security conditions that the security team wants to control. There are
     also various built-in definitions available to control what type of
     resources can be deployed or enforce tags on various resources.
     Apart from the built-in policies, you can also create custom security
     policies. See Figure 7-2.

Home > Policy

Policy | Getting started   ...

Figure 7-2. *Overview of security policies*

In order to implement policy definitions, you need to create them and assign the policies. You can assign these policies using Azure CLI, PowerShell, or the Azure Portal.

– Security policy initiative: Azure policy initiative is a collection of policy definitions or rules that are grouped together for a specific goal. This simplifies the management of policies by grouping policies together into a single item. It also helps ensure the security requirements of the regulators. Figure 7-3 shows an example overview of the security initiatives.

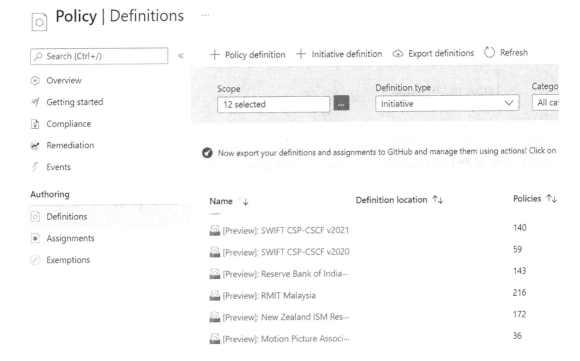

Figure 7-3. *Overview of security initiative*

– With security initiatives, you can define the desired configurations of the workloads to ensure the security compliance of the company. You can use Azure Policy to manage policies and initiatives and assign them to subscriptions or management groups.

- Security recommendations: Defender for cloud periodically analyzes the compliance status of the resources to identify potential security misconfigurations and weakness. Azure Defender for cloud also provides recommendations to fix these security issues. These recommendations mainly come by validating the policies against the resources that don't meet the requirements. See Figure 7-4.

- You can take required actions based on the recommendations from the Defender cloud. Each recommendation has the following information:

- Short description

- Steps to implement the recommendation

- Impacted resources

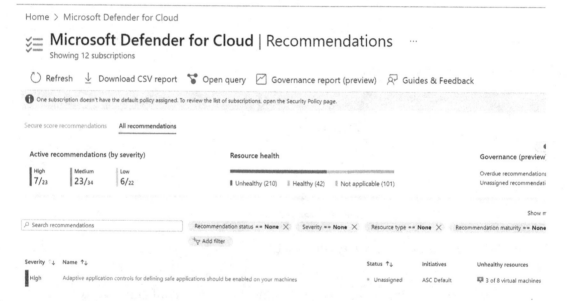

Figure 7-4. Recommendations by Defender for cloud

The main goals of Microsoft Defender are to:

- Understand the current security situation

- Effectively and efficiently improve the security

You can achieve this using the secure score. Defender for cloud checks the cloud resources for security issues and then groups them to determine a single score. See Figure 7-5.

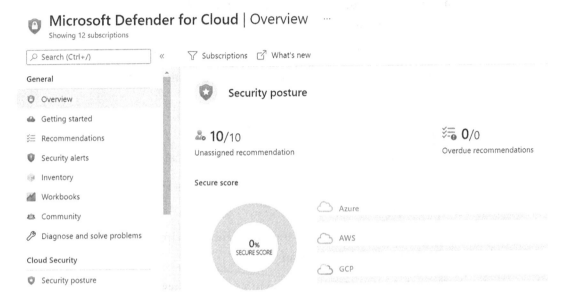

Figure 7-5. *Posture score*

Once you open the overview page of Microsoft Defender for cloud, you can view the secure score for the security posture. The secure score is represented as a percentage.

If you want to understand the score at a granular level, click Explore Security Posture from the Overview page. See Figure 7-6.

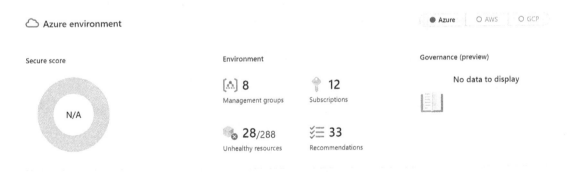

Figure 7-6. *Security posture details*

Advanced Observability

In order to proactively monitor applications, you need to monitor resources to maintain security posture and check the vulnerabilities. You can enable alerts for suspicious activities to find security issues and events.

You need to consider the following points to monitor security related events:

- Use Azure Native tools to monitor the application, infrastructure, and workload

- Create a security operations center or SecOps team

- Monitor the traffic and access requests for the application

- Identify and discover common risks to improve the security score in Microsoft Defender

- Use industry standard protocols and benchmarks to improve the security posture of an organization

- Send logs and alerts to the central log management system

- Enable frequent internal and external audit compliance

- Regularly test security design and implementation

Microsoft Azure provides various monitoring tools to observe the operations and detect behavior:

- Microsoft Defender for cloud: This is a cloud security posture management and cloud workload protection platform for on-premises as well as public cloud resources. See Figure 7-7.

Figure 7-7. *Microsoft Defender for cloud lifecycle*

Defender for cloud maintains the following information to assess your cloud application:

- Defender for cloud secure score: It continuously assesses the security posture so that you can track and improve security efforts.

- Defender for cloud recommendations: It secures the application or workload by providing step-by-step actions that can protect the application from known security risks.

- Defender for cloud alerts: This defends your workload in real-time so your team can act immediately and prevent security events. See Figure 7-8.

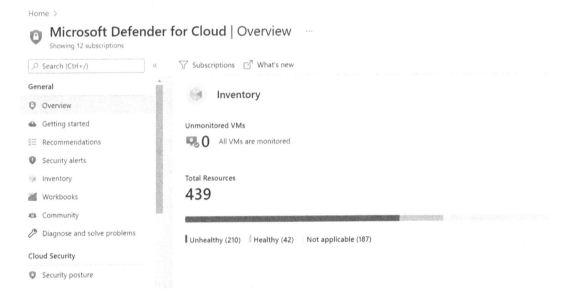

Figure 7-8. *Microsoft Defender for cloud*

- Microsoft Sentinel: Sentinel uses native security information event management (SIEM) and security orchestration solutions in Azure. It provides a bird's eye view across the enterprise to monitor and detect volumes of alerts and resolution of the issues. See Figure 7-9.

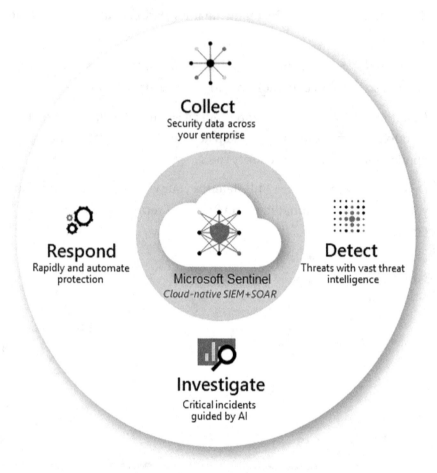

Figure 7-9. *Microsoft Sentinel*

Microsoft Sentinel performs the following activities to improve the overall security of the application. With Microsoft Sentinel, you can perform security orchestration, automation, and response for any security threats:

- Collect data at a scale

- Detect undetected threats if any

- Check threats with artificial intelligence

- Act on the incidents rapidly

- Azure DDOS protection, which mainly focuses on defending against distributed denial of service attacks; see Figure 7-10.

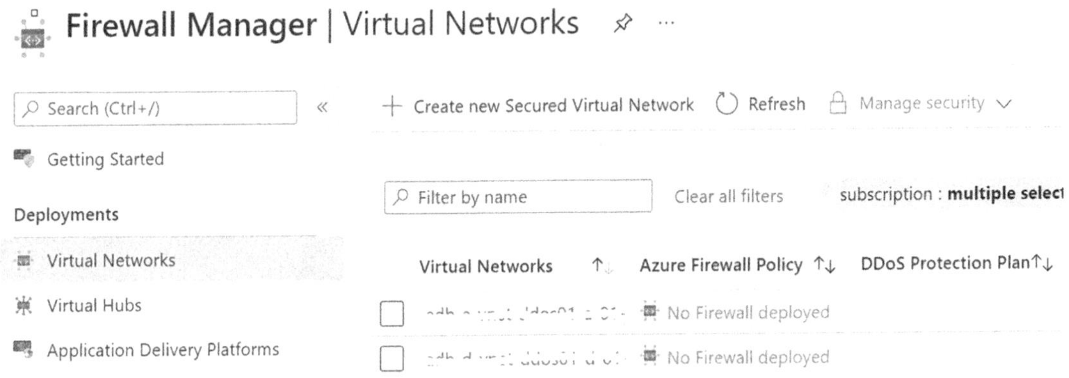

Firewall Manager | Virtual Networks ✗ ...

Search (Ctrl+/) «	+ Create new Secured Virtual Network ◯ Refresh 🔒 Manage security ⌄

Getting Started

Deployments

Filter by name   Clear all filters   subscription : **multiple select**

- Virtual Networks

Virtual Networks ↑	Azure Firewall Policy ↑↓	DDoS Protection Plan↑↓

- Virtual Hubs

☐ ̇̇dh ̇̇ ̇̇ ̇̇ ̇̇ ̇̇dos01 ̇ 01 ̇ 🖥 No Firewall deployed

- Application Delivery Platforms

☐ ̇dh ̇ ̇ ̇ ̇ ̇ ̇ddos01 ̇d ̇ ̇ 🖥 No Firewall deployed

Figure 7-10. *Azure DDOS Protection*

- Azure Rights Management: Protects files and emails across multiple devices.

- Azure Governance Visualizer: Collects insights and information into the policies, and includes role-based access control, Azure blueprints, and subscriptions

Most cloud architecture has compute, networking, data, and identity components and each of these components needs to be monitored closely in terms of security and related issues. Microsoft Defender for cloud has built-in features that monitor the security posture of all these services. You can follow these best practices to configure Microsoft Defender for various services:

- IaaS and PaaS Security: In the IaaS model, you can create various infra services and they will be hosted on Azure. Microsoft Azure provides assurance that the resources will be isolated and security patches and updates will be done in a timely manner. In order to control this in a better manner, you can host the complete IaaS solution on-premises or in a data center. For example, you can create your own virtual network, storage, and host entities. You have a shared responsibility when you consider the reference of PaaS components. See Figure 7-11.

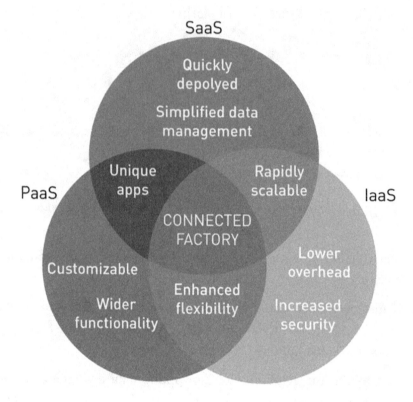

Figure 7-11. *Azure PaaS/SaaS responsibility*

- Virtual machines: For Windows and Linux VMs, use Microsoft
  Defender to take the advantage of free services for missing OS patching, security misconfigurations, and network security. For example,
  virtual machines don't have vulnerability scanning solutions to check
  for security threats. Microsoft Defender for servers watches network
  movement to and from these virtual machines.

Observability means how well you understand what is happening in the system by
collecting logs, metrics, and traces. Observability in the cloud is very hard to achieve.

Azure Monitor

Azure Monitor maximizes the availability and overall performance of the application.
See Figure 7-12.

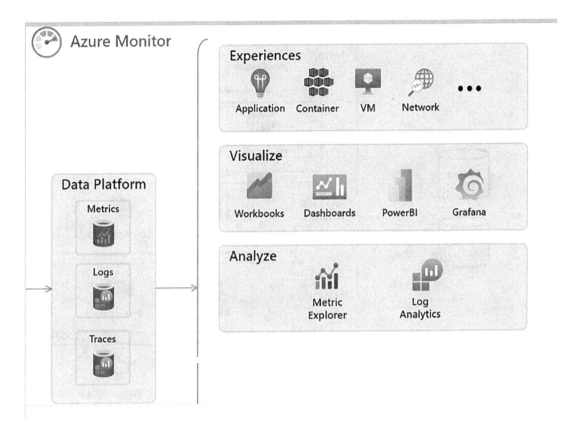

Figure 7-12. Azure Monitor: Applications

All data collected by Azure Monitor is stored in two formats (see Figure 7-13):

– Metrics

– Logs

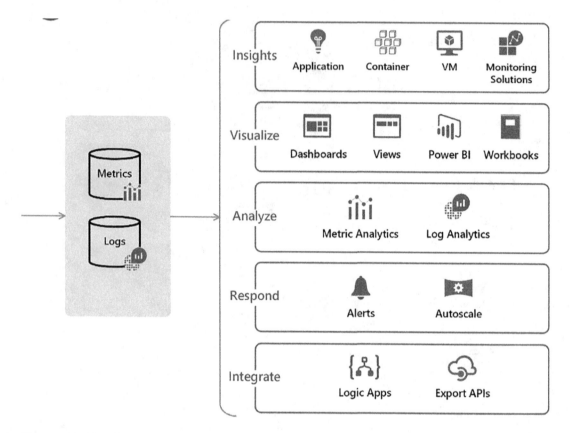

Figure 7-13. *Azure Monitor metrics and logs*

Metrics are numerical values that describe the system at a particular point in time. Metrics are lightweight and efficient and store near real-time logs. Logs contain different kinds of data that is stored in the form of records with sets. For many Azure resources, data is collected by Azure Monitor in the Overview page. For example, you can view the chart and dashboards interactively. See Figure 7-14.

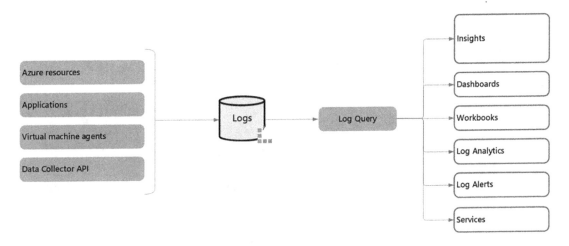

Figure 7-14. *Azure Monitor metrics explorer*

Logs collected by Azure Monitor will be analyzed with queries to get, consolidate, and collect data. You can create and test queries using log analytics. You can use the kusto query language, which is similar to the SQL language, to log queries.

Azure Monitor collects data from various sources. It mainly consists of the following information:

- Application monitoring data: Collects data about the performance and functionality of the source code written on various Azure services.

- Operating system logs: Collect all the logs of the guest operating system data running on Azure, on-premises, or on another public cloud.

- Azure service monitoring data: Contains all the monitoring data from various Azure services.

- Azure subscription monitoring data: Contains all data about the operation and management of the Azure subscription and related information. You can enable diagnostics to extend the data you collect by Azure Monitor. You can also enable logging with Application Insights to collect exceptions, requests, and page views. See Figure 7-15.

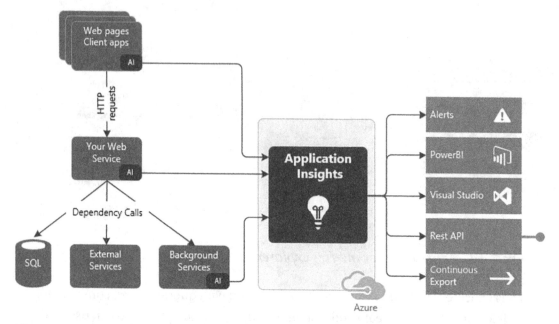

Figure 7-15. *Application Insights*

With Application Insights, you can monitor extensible application performance. Application Insights supports various platforms like .NET, Node.Js, Java, and Python. Application Insights can be used with on-premises or public cloud sources. You can also easily integrate application insights with DevOps processes.

Container Insights monitor the performance of the container workload that's deployed to the Kubernetes cluster. You can improve the performance of the cluster by collecting metrics from controllers, nodes, and containers. Once the container logs are connected, you can enable the monitoring of the Kubernetes clusters. See Figure 7-16.

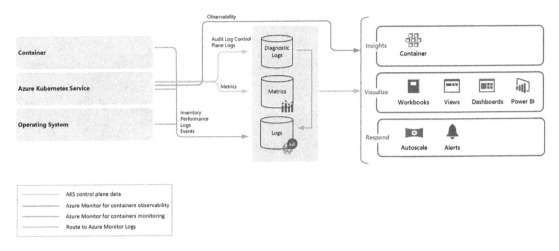

Figure 7-16. *Container Insights*

VM Insights helps organizations monitor the Azure VMs at scale. Overall health and performance are monitored for the Windows and Linux VMs to identify different processes and interdependencies. See Figure 7-17.

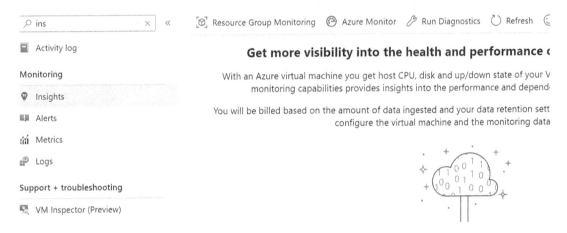

Figure 7-17. *VM Insights*

Alerts in Azure Monitor help detect and address issues before they are identified by end users. See Figure 7-18.

Alert

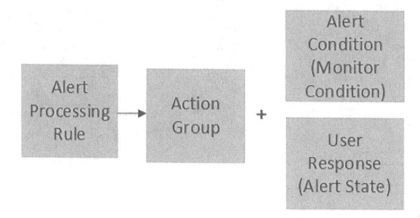

Figure 7-18. *Alerts*

You can create alerts, either on metrics or on log data, based on the Azure Monitor Data platform. Alert rules monitor the operational logs. Alert rules capture the signal and check if the criteria is met. If the conditions are met, an alert will be triggered. See Figure 7-19.

Figure 7-19. *Azure Monitor Alerts*

You can create alert rules using the following combinations:

- Resources to be monitored

- Signal from the resource

- Conditions

Once an alert is triggered, the following sequence of events will unfold:

- The alert processing rule applies the fired alerts. With alert processing rules, you can add or suppress the action groups and apply filters or rules based on a predefined schedule.

- Actions groups trigger the notification based on the workflow to inform the users that alerts have been triggered.

- Notifications methods such as email, SMS, or push notifications

- Automation Runbooks

- Azure functions

- ITSM incidents

- Logic apps

- Webhooks

- Secure webhooks

- Event hubs

- An alert condition is set by the system. When the alert is fired, the alert monitor's condition is set to fired.

Azure Monitor also supports integration with various partners to collect data. With auto-scale, you can set the right amount of resources to handle the application workload. By enabling this feature, you can save on the cost by removing idle resources. While configuring auto-scaling, you can specify the minimum and maximum number of instances and logic to increase or decrease resources. See Figure 7-20.

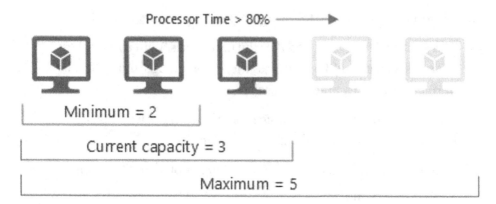

Figure 7-20. *Auto-scaling*

Azure Dashboards allows you to combine different types of data into a single pane. Once the dashboard is ready, you can share it with the end users. For example, you can create a dashboard that combines tiles that shows metrics, activity logs, and the output of the log query. See Figure 7-21.

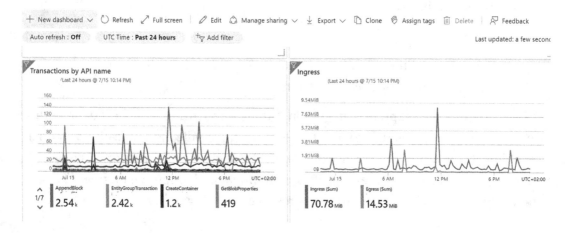

Figure 7-21. *Azure Dashboards*

Azure also has a feature called a *workbook,* which provides a flexible way to perform data analysis and create rich visuals using the Azure Portal. See Figure 7-22.

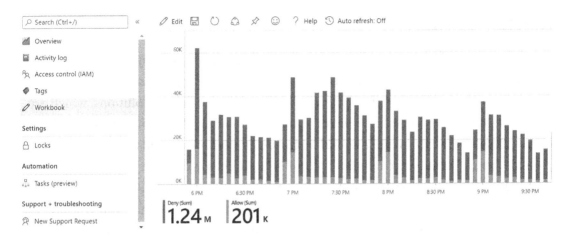

Figure 7-22. *An Azure workbook*

You can use an Azure workbook with Insights or create your own predefined templates.

Power BI is a business analytics service that provides interactive visualizations using various data sources. It is an effective way to make the data available within and outside your organization. You can also automatically import data from Azure Monitor. See Figure 7-23.

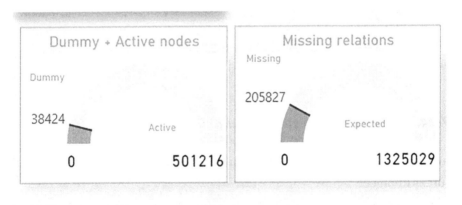

Figure 7-23. *Power BI reports*

Azure Sentinel

Azure Sentinel is a cloud-native, security information, and event management (SIEM) solution, as well as a security orchestration, automation, and response (SOAR) solution.

Microsoft Sentinel has many connectors available for Microsoft solutions, which are out-of the box solutions and provide real-time integration with external tools including Microsoft 365 Defender, Azure AD, and Microsoft Defender for cloud apps. In addition, you can use the REST API to connect various data sources from Azure Sentinel. Microsoft Sentinel can run its workspaces in almost every region where log analytics is generally available. There might be regions where log analytics become generally available and it can take some time for Sentinel to become generally available. See Figure 7-24.

		AZURE STACK HUB	AFRICA	ASIA PACIFIC		AUSTRALIA			BRAZIL
Products	Non-regional	Azure Stack Hub	South Africa North	East Asia	Southeast Asia	Australia Central	Australia East	Australia Southeast	Brazil South
Azure Monitor	✓								
Activity Log	✓								
Metrics	✓								
Diagnostic Logs	✓								
AutoScale			✓	✓	✓	✓	✓	✓	✓
Action Groups	✓								
Alerts	✓								
Alerts (Classic)	✓								
Application Insights			✓	✓	✓	✓	✓	✓	✓
Log Analytics			✓	✓	✓	✓	✓	✓	✓

Figure 7-24. *Azure Sentinel regional availability*

Before you set up Microsoft Sentinel, you need to have the following prerequisites and resources in place:

- – Log analytics workspace

- – Azure subscription

- – Contributor permission for the subscription where you want to deploy Microsoft Sentinel

- – Contributor or reader permission to the resource group

- – Additional permission to connect to the data sources

If you want to enable Microsoft Sentinel, you need to go to the Azure Portal and select the subscription where Sentinel will be created. See Figure 7-25.

Figure 7-25. *Enable Azure Sentinel*

Click the Add button and then select the existing workspace that you want to use or create a new workspace. It is also possible to run Microsoft Sentinel from more than one workspaces, but data is always isolated to a single workspace. See Figure 7-26.

> ## Choose a workspace to add to Microsoft Sentinel
> PREVIEW
>
> ---
>
> 🔍 *Search workspaces*
>
> ---
>
> ➕ Create a new workspace

Figure 7-26. *Enable Azure Sentinel*

Select Add Microsoft Sentinel. Microsoft Sentinel ingests data from various services by connecting services and sending the events and logs to itself. For physical and virtual machines, you can install a log analytics agent, which will collect the logs and forward them to Microsoft Sentinel.

You can also integrate Microsoft Sentinel with various security services. It is empowered by the components that will send the data to the workspace and becomes stronger through interactions. Logs can be ingested directly into Microsoft Sentinel to provide a full picture of events and incidents. For example, Microsoft Sentinel ingests data from other Microsoft services and partner platforms. See Figure 7-27.

193

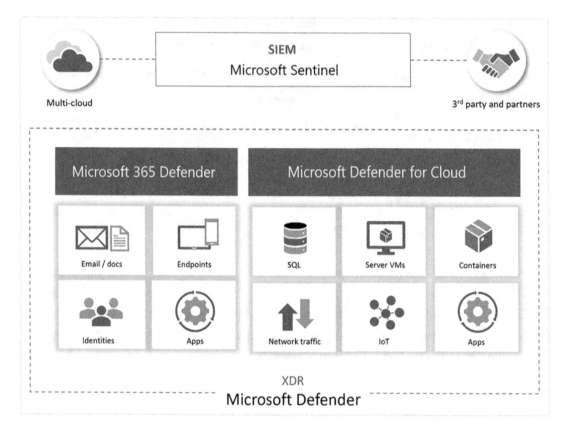

Figure 7-27. *Azure Sentinel with Microsoft Defender*

Apart from sending data, Microsoft Sentinel has various other features:

- Uses information with machine learning

- Creates visualizations with workbooks

- Runs playbooks with alerts

- Integrates with partner platforms

- Integrates and fetches enrichment feeds from threat intelligence platforms

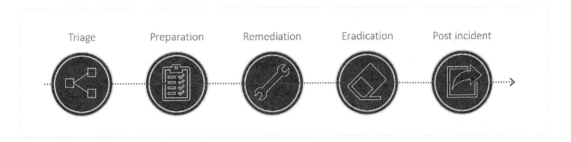

Triage   Preparation   Remediation   Eradication   Post incident

Figure 7-28. *Incident management and response process*

You can also use Microsoft Sentinel to manage incidents and respond to responses in case of failures. See Figures 7-28 and 7-29.

Figure 7-29. *Incident management and response process*

Content in Microsoft Sentinel includes the following:

- Data connectors: Microsoft Sentinel has many out-of-the-box connectors to start ingesting data to Microsoft Sentinel. For example,
  Microsoft 365 Defender connector is a service to the service connector that integrates data from Office 365, Azure AD, and so on. See
  Figure 7-30.

Incident Response Lifecycle

Figure 7-30. *Azure Sentinel connectors*

- Parsers: These parsers provide log formatting in the Advanced
  Security Information Model (ASIM) formats to support their use
  across Microsoft Sentinel.

- Workbooks: These provide monitoring, visualization, and interactiv-
  ity with data using Microsoft Sentinel. See Figure 7-31.

Figure 7-31. *Workbooks visualization*

- Hunting queries: These queries are used by the Security Operations
  Team (SOC) team to hunt for threats in Microsoft Sentinel. See
  Figure 7-32.

Figure 7-32. Microsoft Sentinel hunting queries

Hunting dashboards provide built-in, ready-made queries to get started and familiar with tables and query language. Queries run on the data stored in the log tables. These built-in queries are developed by the Microsoft security researchers. See Figure 7-33.

Figure 7-33. Microsoft Sentinel hunting custom queries

You can also create custom queries or modify existing queries and then share them with users who belong to the same tenant.

To create a new query, select New Query and then select Create. Click the Create Entity Mapping and then select the entity type, identifiers, and columns.

Typical hunting queries start with the table or parser name followed by the operators, separated by the pipe character. See Figure 7-34.

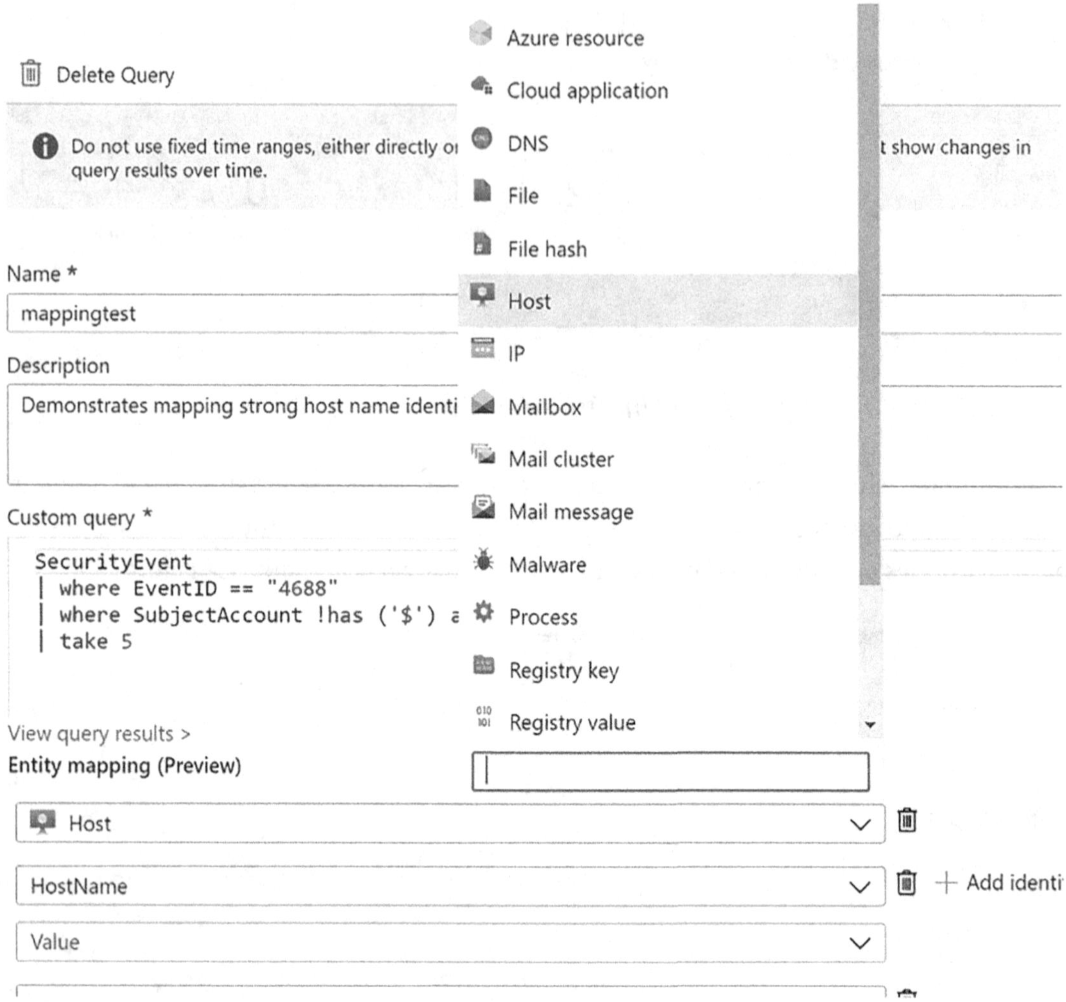

🗑 Delete Query

ⓘ Do not use fixed time ranges, either directly or   t show changes in
   query results over time.

Name *

mappingtest

Description

Demonstrates mapping strong host name identi

Custom query *

```
SecurityEvent
| where EventID == "4688"
| where SubjectAccount !has ('$') a
| take 5
```

View query results >

Entity mapping (Preview)

| 🖥 Host | ∨ | 🗑 |

| HostName | ∨ | 🗑 + Add identi |

| Value | ∨ |

Dropdown list:
- 🔷 Azure resource
- ☁ Cloud application
- 🌐 DNS
- 📄 File
- 📄 File hash
- 🖥 Host
- ▦ IP
- ✉ Mailbox
- 📧 Mail cluster
- 📨 Mail message
- 🐞 Malware
- ⚙ Process
- ▦ Registry key
- 010 Registry value
  101

Figure 7-34. Microsoft Sentinel hunting create new queries

— Playbooks and Azure Logic App custom connector: This provides
features for the automated investigations, remediations, and
response scenarios in Microsoft Sentinel. Playbooks in Microsoft
Sentinel are based on workflows, like Azure logic apps, which can be
used to schedule, automate, and orchestrate workflow across the
enterprise.

Azure Logic app communicates with other systems and services using these connectors:

- Custom connectors

- Managed connectors

- Microsoft Sentinel connectors

- Triggers

- Actions

- Dynamic fields

Conclusion

This chapter explained how to secure data stored in the cloud and how to provide secure access to that data. You also learned about the various ways to classify data and make it available for downstream users and applications in a secure manner. Finally, you also learned about the various data encryption patterns and related models used while working with public cloud providers, such as Azure, Google, AWS, and so on.

CHAPTER 8

Creating a Security Culture

Every organization across every industry should take information security seriously. Security attacks can take place nearly every day and can result in exposing applications to the outside world. By establishing a strong culture of cybersecurity, enterprise organizations lay a foundation that leads to decreased number of threats in the long run.

The previous chapter covered automated security monitoring, including setting up a security policy using Azure Monitor and Azure Sentinel.

This chapter covers the following topics:

- Leadership support

- Training

Leadership Support

Organizations need a leader, someone who is responsible for creating a culture of security. Building a security culture must be handled as a project, with support from the highest level of executives. Enterprise organizations can start by executing these steps:

- Recruiting the right people to run the program

- Determining the project scope

- Measuring the security awareness and interests in the organization

- Creating actions of execution to reach goals

- Creating deadlines for different actions to determine the start and end dates

© Sagar Lad 2023
S. Lad, *Azure Security For Critical Workloads*, https://doi.org/10.1007/978-1-4842-8936-5_8

- Defining metrics

- Creating success factors

Establishing a security culture across an enterprise organization creates an environment where management and employees speak the same language and have a common understanding of their own business and strategy. A security culture must be built together with the employees.

People, processes, and technologies are often seen as the three pillars of information security. Although a proper balance between the three is essential, the aspects of internal culture and training as they relate to the "people" pillar are often overlooked. Not focusing on the people in an organization leads to reduced effectiveness of processes and technologies. See Figure 8-1.

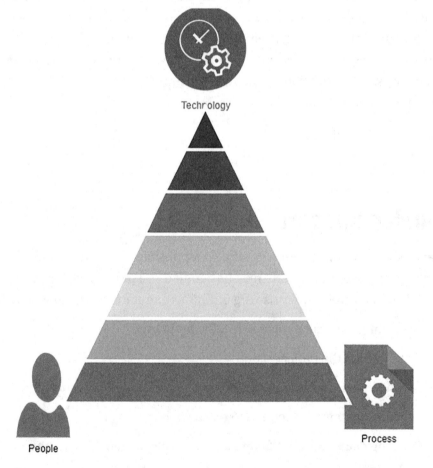

Figure 8-1. *Security culture: people, processes, and technologies*

Organizations should seek to establish a culture where employees understand the importance of cybersecurity and define policies, procedures, and controls. Modifying the existing corporate culture to incorporate security awareness will require support from the leaders of the following items:

- Encourage the initiative to create security culture: Stakeholders within the organizations should promote a security awareness culture to maintain a positive attitude toward information security. Support for security measures expected by the enterprise will help the company achieve their goals. In addition to that, business managers should look for employees who are not working with the right attitude and help create a positive and proactive environment.

- Lead by example: Regardless of what leaders tell employees, if they don't follow the defined processes, policies, and controls then it will create the wrong impression among the employees and they will become less serious about the security culture.

- Fundamental understanding of the information security: Stakeholders in the organization may not be security experts, but they should be provided with additional training to get a foundational understanding and knowledge of security. Having basic knowledge of security among the employees and between the leaders can mitigate the possibility of individuals involved in security incidents.

- Proactive leadership involvement: Stakeholders in the organization should create a proactive plan for an incident response plan, business continuity plan, and other key procedures. Every stakeholder might not be aware of the procedures, but being aware about such information allows leaders to contribute to the organization.

A security awareness culture will encourage employees to question skeptical activities, become more resilient to social engineering attacks, and adhere to the defined policies, procedures, and controls. See Figure 8-2.

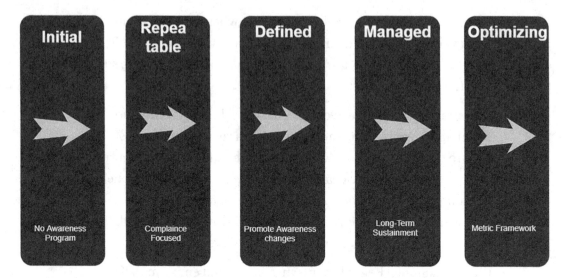

Figure 8-2. *Security culture: people, processes, and technologies*

All the teams in the enterprise organization can run a mix of technical, administrative, and professional programs to improve overall security. Let's look into a few of the possible initiatives that enterprise organizations can follow:

- Gap Analysis: First, you need to understand the existing gap analysis, which is where the organization stands today. By performing the gap analysis, you can easily find what needs to be done and when.

- Needs differ for each department: Different departments and disciplines have different needs as per their knowledge and skills. It is also advised to run the safety program to create an iterative culture building process across the departments so that it is easier to see if such a safety program has the desired effect.

- Improve security competence: You can perform many activities to spread awareness across the organization to improve the overall security. Metrics should be defined for each activity to understand if the goal has been achieved or not and to improve the overall security competence.

- Games: Cost and complexity of developing games today is lower than ever. We can create both computer games as well as board games related to security awareness and quiz to improve security awareness.

- Ethical hacking: Hire a company that can test physical security, employee goodwill, and your public-facing systems to avoid phishing attacks.

Training

In order to improve the overall security culture and security awareness, you should train employees and keep them up-to-date about possible security issues and how to avoid them.

- Be flexible to the corporate culture: Creating a security culture differs not only from organization to organization but also within the departments and management levels.

- Instead of creating a fixed path to drive security training across the organization, it is better to sit together with senior stakeholders and employees and create a security awareness program.

- Validate training to achieve organizational goals: Phishing attacks, data breaches, and CEO fraud attacks are the major concerns by most practitioners across the world. Undertrained employees lack the ability to detect security threats and don't have a correct understanding of a security attack. Be ready to focus not only on the best training but also to train for all possible scenarios.

- Replicate phishing scenarios at random intervals: Phishing simulation techniques are really important for maintaining the workforce's phishing defense. Simulating phishing scenarios will enable organizations to understand and predict employee behavior against the attack and track behavioral changes over time.

- Frequency of the training: Security training should happen often, to keep security a top priority for everyone. Although there is no magic frequency for such training, short trainings distributed frequently are most effective and best able to create a security culture across an organization. See Figure 8-3.

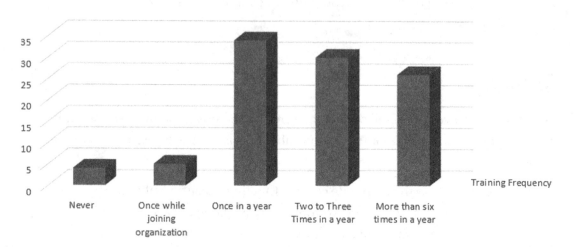

Figure 8-3. *Security training frequency*

- Focus on employee's behavioral changes: Security professionals view technical infrastructure as a more useful tool for avoiding security incidents rather than creating security-aware training. It is impossible to replace security training with the technical controls. Physical infrastructure is great at preventing security attacks until a phishing email comes into an employee's inbox. It is worth considering security training as the outcome of behavioral changes rather than as a compliance requirement. This behavioral change is not the ultimate goal of the training, but it is measurable. Focus on the phishing rates, number of employees who report to an email, and events blocked by the endpoint protection to back security awareness with data. See Figure 8-4.

Figure 8-4. *Security training vs physical infrastructure*

- Keep faith in employees to tackle security challenges: Security professionals report low confidence in the company's employees and stakeholders to handle phishing attacks. Having limited confidence in employees' ability to handle security threats makes it important to treat security incidents as an opportunity rather than showcasing them as the inability of employees to tackle security issues.

Conclusion

This chapter explored how to create a security culture across your organization with the support and vision from the stakeholders and organizational leaders. In addition to this, you have to train employees across your organization to be able to recognize and tackle security challenges.

Index

A

Access control, 124–126

Access tokens, 26, 29, 32, 34

Active Directory Federation Service, 63
- authentication and authorization, 43
- authentication methods, 45, 46, 48
- on-premises, 44
- secured identity federation, 43

Ad Hoc configuration protocols (AHCP), 69

Advanced security information model (ASIM), 196

Advanced threat protection (ATP), 128, 129

Application development team, 135

Application insight, 90, 91

Application layer principles, 17

Application proxy connector, 50, 54

Application security
- availability, 113
- Azure AD multifactor authentication, 116
- BYOD, 111
- confidentiality, 112
- identity management, 115, 116
- integrity, 113
- layered security approach, 112
- security layers, 113–115
- zero trust cloud security, 112

Application security group (ASG), 76–78

Architecture roots, 14

ARM template deployment, 90

Asynchronous/synchronous communication, 12

Authentication flow, 31

Authorization server, 31–34

Azure active directory, 21, 25, 98

Azure Active directory security model, 25, 35, 63

Azure AD application proxy
- components, 51
- with conditional access, 51
- features, 50
- on-premises web applications, 50, 51
- remote users access, 51
- secure and remote access, 49
- use cases, 52
- workflow, 53, 54

Azure AD Business 2 Business collaboration (Azure AD B2B), 54, 55

Azure AD business to customers (Azure AD B2C), 56, 57

Azure AD federated authentication, 47

Azure AD federation service, 44

Azure AD multifactor authentication, 116

Azure AD password protection, 38

Azure AD PIM roles, 59

Azure AD security defaults, 37

Azure AD security model
- hybrid identity, 35
- identity assessment score, 35
- secure organizations checklist, 35

Azure Advisor, 92

Azure AD with password hash sync, 45

Printed in the United States
by Baker & Taylor Publisher Services